DEFENSE OF THE SEVEN SACRAMENTS

Henry VIII,
King of England
King of Ireland

Translated by: Rev. Louis O'Donovan, STL
Edited by: D.P. Curtin

DEFENSE OF THE SEVEN SACRAMENTS

Library of Congress Cataloging-in-Publication Data

17th century woodcut of the late royal court of King Henry VIII

DEFENSE OF THE SEVEN SACRAMENTS

DEFENSE OF THE SEVEN SACRAMENTS

Table of Contents:

DEFENSE OF THE SEVEN SACRAMENTS

DEFENSE OF THE SEVEN SACRAMENTS

Every Person in the least conversant with ecclesiastical History, or indeed with the civil History of England, must know that Martin Luther himself, remarkable a Man as he was, was not more so than the royal Author of the following Work: Nor can a Reader of either Species of History be unacquainted with those fatal Confusions, Animosities and Devastations, that were consequent of, and owed their Rise to, that Mode of Religion introduced by the former, and in a great Measure established by the latter in these three Kingdoms.

We shall not enter into a Detail, at large of those Springs and Motives that were the efficient Cause of the Reformation (as it is called) in the old Religion: We shall only observe, very briefly, that, antecedently to that most remarkable Revolution, some of the Clergy, sunk in that Sloth which great Affluence is but too apt to generate in the human Mind, became so relaxed in Discipline, and in the Duties in general of their holy Profession, that there was a real Necessity for a Reformation of Manners. Pampered Sloth not only begets a Looseness of Morals, but is often the Father of Ignorance; and thus, too many of the sacred Order, not only did not practice, but were really, even in Speculation and Knowledge, Strangers to their Duty. The few (comparatively the few) Learned and Virtuous saw and lamented the almost general Depravity of the Times; and it is probable that Luther, at first, meant no more than to expose and correct the Enormities which he everywhere saw practiced: But, puffed up with a Conceit of his own Abilities; (which indeed were far from being contemptible) he, from endeavoring to reform particular Abuses, which no way concerned the Essence of Religion, (though they threw a Stain on many of its Members) at length set about a Reformation of Religion itself; and came to think his own Knowledge in Divinity superior to that of the whole aggregate Church. The Ambition of, and Contests between some of the Germanic Princes, concerning Matters of a civil Nature, were favorable to his Views; and, in the Career of his newly-broached Opinions, inconsistent as they were, one with the other, he prevailed so far as to engage the Power of Magistracy in their Propagation and Defense. All Europe stood astonished, when it beheld Armies of military Apostles enforcing an Obedience to the wild and incoherent Notions of a vain, obstinate, self-willed and enthusiastic Clergyman. The People that were determined not to quit the old Road to Heaven, thought themselves obliged to defend the ancient Religion, by the like Means; and thus, a general Warfare sprang, from the Petulancy and fiery Zeal of an Individual. The learned and virtuous Part of the Clergy employed their Zeal, and exerted their Talents, on this alarming Occasion; and demonstrated to the World, that the Deviations from good Morals could be no just Foundation for a Separation from that Religion, which had the Promise of Christ for its Support and Existence, whilst the World should last.

Henry the Eighth was a Prince of great Learning, considering the Age in which he lived. He had well studied both Philosophy and Divinity, in his Youth; his Father, Henry the Seventh, having intended him for the ecclesiastical State. His Writings against Luther, (I mean the following Work, so much approved of by Pope Leo the Tenth) shew a Fund of ecclesiastical Erudition, and a Strength of Understanding, uncommon in Persons of his high Station. It must, indeed, be acknowledged, that they breathe too much of the Spirit of Acrimony, and run into a Latitude of Abuse, ever disgustful to Readers of Taste, Moderation and Candour: But let it be remembered, at the same Time, That extreme Virulency, Insolence and Self-sufficiency, almost everywhere, mark the Writings of Luther and his Fellow-reformers: That those Reformers having thus led the Way, their Opponents thought themselves justified in retaliating the Abuse, with which they had been attacked: And that the Manners of those distant Times, wherein polemical Disputes about Religion were so strongly and warmly agitated, differ very widely from those of the present more enlightened and more moderate Age.

Luther was not less inflamed, by the Censure of the University of Paris (a), to whose Judgment he had submitted his Writings, with great Elogies, and who had condemned his Doctrine in above an hundred

Propositions; than he was to find that the King of England had written against him. His Answer abounds with (b) "heinous Affronts and injurious Lies, in almost every Page. This Writing did its Author no Honor, even among those of his own Party; even his Friends were scandalized at the injurious Contempt, with which he treated all that was most august in the Universe, and at the whimsical Manner, in which he judged of Points of Doctrine."

Henry was a pious and zealous Roman Catholic, until such Times as he suffered himself to be borne away by an immoderate Passion for Women, and found his Solicitations at Rome for a Divorce from his Queen, Katherine of Aragon, absolutely fruitless. Then it was that he broke all Measures with the Holy See; and he, who had been a powerful and firm Defender of the Church, became the Cornerstone, in England, of that Reformation which he had so warmly and strenuously opposed.

*Notwithstanding this Falling-off, however, his 'Defense of the Seven Sacraments' is a Work of considerable Merit. Its Orthodoxy we cannot doubt of, when we read the Pope's Bull, granting him the most honorable and glorious Title of **DEFENDER OF THE FAITH**; a Title still retained by his Successors on the Throne, though of a contrary Religion. Although it is not to be doubted but that subsequent Writers have handled the Subject-matter of this Book with more Accuracy, Clearness and Precision; yet the Work before us may not only be very profitably perused, but is also extremely curious, when we consider its Author s very remarkable and inconsistent Character. The London Edition, from whence the present is taken, has been carefully corrected throughout, in the Orthography and Punctuation, and the Text, obscure in some Parts, hath been elucidated, without deviating, however, from the Sense of the Author. Upon the Whole, we may venture to affirm, that this Edition is vastly preferable to all former Ones, in the English Tongue; and we flatter ourselves with the Hope, that the Pains we have taken, in the Publication of a Work, hitherto so extremely scarce, will be satisfactory to the Curious.*

Letter to Pope Leo
On the Subject of the "Hesertio"

Most Holy Father: I most humbly commend myself to you, and devoutly kiss your blessed feet. Whereas we believe that no duty is more incumbent on a Catholic sovereign than to preserve and increase the Christian faith and religion and the proofs thereof, and to transmit them preserved thus inviolate to posterity, by his example in preventing them from being destroyed by any assailant of the faith or in any wise impaired, so when we learned that the pest of Martin Luther s heresy had appeared in Germany and was raging everywhere, without let or hindrance, to such an extent that many, infected with its poison, were falling away, especially those whose furious hatred rather than their zeal for Christian truth had prepared them to believe all its subtleties and lies, we were so deeply grieved at this heinous crime of the German nation (for whom we have no light regard), and for the sake of the Holy Apostolic See, that we bent all our thoughts and energies on up-rooting in every possible way, this cockle, this heresy from the Lord s flock. When we perceived that this deadly venom had advanced so far and had seized upon the weak and ill-disposed minds of so many that it could not easily be overcome by a single effort, we deemed that nothing could be more efficient in destroying the contagion than to declare these errors worthy of condemnation, after they had been examined by a convocation of learned and scholarly men from all parts of our realm. This course of action we likewise recommended to a number of others. In the first place, we earnestly entreated His Imperial Majesty, through our fraternal love for him, and all the electoral princes, to bethink them of their Christian duty and their lofty station and to destroy this pernicious man, together with his scandalous and heretical publications, after his refusal to return to God. But convinced that, in our ardor for the welfare of Christendom, in our zeal for the Catholic faith and our devotion to the Apostolic See, we had not yet done enough, we determined to show by our own writings our attitude towards Luther and our opinion of his vile books; to manifest more openly to all the world that we shall ever defend and uphold, not only by force of arms but by the resources of our intelligence and our services as a Christian, the Holy Roman Church. For this reason, we have thought that this first attempt of our modest ability and learning could not be more worthily dedicated than to your Holiness, both as a token of our filial reverence and an acknowledgment of your careful solicitude for the weal of Christendom. We feel assured that our first fruits will be enhanced in value if it be approved by the whole some judgment of your Blessedness. May you live long and happily!

From our royal palace at Greenwich,
the twenty-first day of May 1521.
Your Holiness' most devoted and humble son,

Henry
by the grace of God King of England
and France, and Lord of Ireland.

Oration of John Clark
for Henry, King of England and France, Lord of Ireland, Defender of the Faith

Most Holy Father:

What great Troubles have been stirred up, by the pernicious Opinions of Martin Luther; which of late Years first sprung out of the lurking Holes of the Hussitanian Heresy, in the School of Wittenberg in Germany; from thence spreading themselves over most Parts of the Christian World; how many unthinking Souls they have deceived, and how many Admirers and Adherents they have met with; because these are all Things very well known ; and because, in this Place, a Medium is more requisite, than Prolixity; I care not for relating. Truly, although many of Luther s Works are most impiously, by his Libels, spread abroad in the World: Yet none of them seems more execrable, more venomous, and more pernicious to Mankind, than That, entitled, The Babylonian Captivity of the Church; in refuting which, many grave and learned Men have diligently labored.

My most serene and invincible Prince, Henry VIII. King of England, France and Ireland, and most affectionate Son of Your Holiness, and of the sacred Roman Church, hath written a Book against this Work of Luther's, which he has dedicated to Your Holiness; and hath commanded me to offer, and deliver the same; which I here present: But before You receive it, most holy Father, may it please You, that I speak Somewhat of the Devotion and Veneration of my King towards Your Holiness, and this most Holy See; as also, of the other Reasons which moved him to publish this Work. Nor is it amiss to take Notice, in this Place, of this horrid and furious Monster; as also of his Stings and Poisons, whereby he intends to infect the whole World, and to delineate him before Your Holiness in his own proper Colors; that the more formidable the Enemy is, and the greater the Danger appears, the more glorious may the Triumph shew when that is overcome, and this removed. But, O immortal God! what bitter Language! what so hot and inflamed Force of Speaking can be in vented, sufficient to declare the Crimes of that most filthy Villain, who has undertaken to cut in Pieces the seamless Coat of Christ, and to disturb the quiet State of the Church of God! When, like an excellent Esteemer of Things, he attributes to Your Holiness no more Power in the Church of God, than to any of the least Priests amongst the People; but, like a third Cato, fallen from Heaven, most unseasonably condemns the Behavior of all the Ministers in the Church; calls Rome a Sinner, wretched, an Adulteress; and lastly, Babylon itself! He accuses Your Holiness of Heresy, and makes himself (thrice Apostate) as often as there is Question in the Explication of the Christian Faith; equal in Authority to St. Peter, Prince of the Apostles! And that he may the better demonstrate himself as great an Enemy to Religion, as to Manners, his most impure Hands have burnt the Decrees and most holy Statutes of the Fathers, in which were contained the true Discipline of a good Life. And, as one most audacious, leaving Nothing attempted; he at last publishes this Book of the Babylonian Captivity. In which, good God! What and how prodigious Poison, what deadly Bane, how much consuming and mortal Venom this poisonous Serpent has spewed out, not only against the wicked Manners of our Age, which in some Manner might have been borne with; not only against Your Holiness, but also against Your Office; against ecclesiastical Hierarchy, this See, and against that Rock established by God himself: finally, against the whole Body of the Church of God! Here, the Bond of Chastity is broken, holy Fasts, religious Vows, Rites, Ceremonies, Worship of God, Solemnity at Mass, et cetera, are abolished, and ex terminated, by the strangest Perfidiousness that ever was heard of. This man institutes Sacraments after his own Fancy, reducing them to three, to two, to one; and that One he handles so pitifully, that he seems to be about the reducing of it at last to Nothing at all. O Height of Impiety! O most abominable and most execrable Villainy of Man! What intolerable Blasphemies, from an Heap of Calumnies and Lies, without any Law, Method, or Order, does he utter against God, and his Servants, in this Book! Socrates, a Man judged by Apollo's Oracle, to be the wisest of Men, was by the Athenians poisoned for disputing against the commonly-received Opinion they had of God, and against that Religion which was at that Time taught to be the best on Earth. Could this Destroyer of Christian Religion expect any better from true Christians, for his extreme Wickedness against God? But indeed, he did not look on it; who, when dreading Punishment (which he well deserved) fled, with a Mischief, into his perpetual lurking Holes in Bohemia, the Mother and Nurse of his Heresies. If he had remained, and had not by Your Holiness been prohibited the free dispersing abroad of his Errors; what Danger, what devouring Conflagration this Plague had brought to all Christendom; let the Hussitanian Heresy evince; which though, contented at first with small Beginnings, yet, through the Neglect of Superiors, increased to such a Height, that at last it turned, not only Cities, and People, but also that most populous Kingdom of Bohemia, from the Christian Faith; reducing it to that Misery, under which it now languishes. What can we think would be the End of this raging Mischief, which is carried on with such Violence and unbridled Fury, in his Precludiums, as he calls them; as if some Erynnis were sent from Hell in a Trice to confound all before it, and so rapidly transported, as if it would seem to leave Nothing whereon to exercise future Fury? which, tracing the Steps of the Hussites, has added so much Poison to them, that now the Enemy appears more formidable, by how much more he equalizes all Arch-heretics in his Doctrine, and surpasses them in his malicious and wicked Intentions: Indeed, the Danger is also so much the greater, as it is easier to add worse Proceedings to bad Beginnings, than to begin 111; and to increase Inventions, then to invent. But Your Holiness, most blessed Father, has circumspectly taken Care of your Flock; and meeting the Smoak, ready to break into open Conflagration and Flame, omitted Nothing that might avail to the preventing so great Evils; or at first to the Reconciliation of their Author; afterwards to his Punishment and Extermination. The great Indignity of this Matter, as also Your Holiness, and the King my Master's Letters, moved the Emperor to send this Man, swelled with Contumelies, into Exile. Learned Men, on all Sides, have in their Works opposed themselves, as so many Bucklers, for the Christian Faith, against the Darts of this pernicious Reprobate.

Let others speak of other Nations, certainly my Britainy (called England by our modern Cosmographers) situated in the furthermost End of the World, and separated from the Continent by the Ocean; as it hath never been behind in the Worship of God, and true Christian Faith, and due Obedience to the Roman Church; either to Spain,, France,

Germany, or Italy; nay, to Rome itself; so likewise, there is no Nation which more impugns this Monster, and the Heresies broached by him, and which more condemns, and detests them. In which Sort of most excellent Praise, I can prefer none to him, whom I have now recorded, King Henry, Your Holiness s most devoted Son; who, as soon as he understood, that the Dignity of that Government, illustrated by Your Integrity and Virtue, and enlarged by Your great Actions; was, together with the Universal Church, so bitterly inveighed against, by this Son of Perdition; not only undertook this pious Work himself, whereby he has learnedly confuted the Errors of this impious Man; but likewise the most learned Clergy of this Realm, have, to the utmost of their Powers, endeavored, with all Diligence, to remove from the Hearts of the People all Doubts, Fears and Scruples, that might in any wise happen to possess, or trouble the Minds of the weaker Sort; so that, amongst us, the Church of God is in great Tranquility; no Differences, no Disputes, no ambiguous Words, Murmurings or Complaints, are heard amongst the People: All Troubles of Mind, all Renovations in the World, all vain Horror of Antichrist s Reign, are now vanished.

But now, lest my Discourse may seem too prolix, or tedious to the diligent Attention Your Holiness is pleased to give; I shall presently come to a Conclusion.

Only first be pleased, that I declare the Reason that moved my most serene King to undertake this Work. For I believe it will cause Admiration in several, that a Prince, so much busied with the Cares of his own Kingdom, both at home and abroad ; and whose Affairs afford him so little Respite, should undertake such Things, as, according to the common Saying, might require to employ wholly all the Thoughts of a Man, and indeed, of such a one, as is no novice neither ; but rather for his whole Time experienced in the Studies of Learning: Yet, notwithstanding all this, he that considers his great Actions done for the Faith of Christ, and his accustomed Reverence towards this holy See, will not think it so strange that he, who, with his Forces and revenged Sword, has formerly defended the Church of Rome, when in greatest Dangers and Calamities of Wars; should now, for the Glory of God, and Tranquility of the Roman Church, by his Ingenuity and Pen, put a Stop to Heresies, which so endanger the Catholic Faith.

If no sincere Christian could suffer so great Evils to creep into the Church, without opposing all his Forces and Studies against them; what ought not a Prince to do, and such a Prince, as, by divine Providence, is advanced to that Honor and Dignity, as it were, for that very Cause, that he might protect the Catholic Faith, and maintain the Christian Religion inviolable from all pestilential Endeavors?

Shall we admire, that Piety should extort from him (being both a Christian and a Prince,) what is but the Duty of every Christian? These, most holy Father, are the chief Reasons of his entering upon this Work; his accustomed Veneration to Your Holiness; Christian Piety in the Cause of God; and a royal Grief and Indignation of seeing Religion trodden under Foot. I confess the Desire of Glory might have been able to have induced him to these Things ; that as he, who, under the Charge of the best Tutors, and a Father none of the most indulgent, having passed his younger Days in good Learning, and afterwards so well versed in Holy Scriptures, that confiding in his own Abilities, he often, (not without great Glory) disputed with the most Learned in Britain; might now also, for Glory s Sake, fight in the Field of Learning against Martin Luther; a Man indeed not illiterate.

Nor do I see in what else he could, with more Glory and Applause, have employed this Treasure of Knowledge; a Talent, doubtless, given him by God himself for this very End. But yet the pious Prince himself does modestly acknowledge, in his Preface, how little he at tributes to the Force of his own Wit, which is so much esteemed by others: For, excusing his Insufficiency in Learning, in that Preface, he arrogates no more to himself, than to confess that this Task might have been much better performed by many others; and that he himself, (much unfit, confiding only in the Assistance of the divine Goodness) had, through the Instigation of Piety, and Grief of seeing Religion so much abused, at tempted to discover, by Reason, the Lutheran Heresies: Not that he thought it honorable to contend with Luther, who is so much despised, hissed at, and cried down over the whole World; but that, amongst other Things, he might testify to the World what his Opinion was of this prodigious Monster, and his Followers; thinking himself concerned to publish that in Writing, not so much, lest Scruples of Conscience should follow his Silence, as, by his Example, to induce others to the like Undertakings, who had received a richer Gift of Science from the Giver of Light. I confess what the Godly Prince has writ against the Errors of Luther might compel Luther himself (if he had the least Spark of Christian Piety in him) to recant his Heresies, and recall again the straying and almost forlorn Flock, not only from Errors, but from Hell itself, where it miserably runs head-long. But what can be done, where Pharaoh s Heart is hardened; where the Wound stinks with Putrefaction; where Wickedness, Lying to itself, is become miserable? being unwilling to hear that it should understand, or to understand that it should do well. The Change of his Mind, and altering his Councils to better, must be a great Miracle of Almighty God; for what learned Men have writ against him as yet, does but only irritate him to grow every Day worse and worse. Truly, my most serene King is so far from expecting any Good from this Idol and vain Phantom, that he rather thinks this raging and mad Dog is not to be dealt with by Words, there being no Hopes of his Conversion, but with drawn Swords, Cannons, and other Habiliments of War; (such as he would use against the Turks themselves; if Time permitted,) that, being constrained by due Punishment, he might be reduced, if not to Amendment, at least to Fear. And because, most Holy Father, the King could not revenge with the Sword, God s Cause and Yours; He takes other Arms, and enters the Field of Learning; not in this Kind of Combat, like another Hercules, to fight against this Hydra; but because this Viper s Madness rages nowhere more to the Dishonor of God, than in his Book of the Babylonian Captivity; nor seems he, anywhere else, by his deceitful Arguments, more to endanger weaker Judgments. Having therefore begun to batter down this Work, he assaults it with the Force and Engines of his Arguments; therein performing the Office of a pious, magnanimous General, whose Duty in military Discipline, is to supply his Soldiers with most Auxiliaries, where the Enemy presses on with greatest force. Which Work of his, though it had the Approbation of the most Learned of his Kingdom; yet he resolved not to publish until Your Holiness (from whom we ought to receive the Sense of the Gospel, by Your quick and most sublime Judgment) deem it worthy to pass through the Hands of Men. May therefore Your Holiness take in good Part, and graciously accept this little Book, sent and submitted to Your Examination: In which, the pious, and Your most devoted Prince, has, with all his Power, endeavored to procure, in some

Manner, that weaker Understandings should not be drawn out of the Way, by the most wicked Works of this perverse Man ; and hopes so to have acquitted himself, as at least he may appear to have demonstrated his Veneration towards the Christian religion, and towards Your Holiness.

DEFENSE OF THE SEVEN SACRAMENTS

We receive this Book with great Joy: Truly it is such, as nothing could have been sent more acceptable to Us, and our venerable Brethren. But, indeed, we know not whether more to praise, or to admire, that most potent, prudent and truly most Christian King; who, with his Sword, has totally subdued the Enemies of Christ's Church, Enemies, who like the Heads of the Hydra, often cut off, and forthwith growing up again;) have often endeavored to tear in Pieces the seamless Coat of Christ; and, at Length, the Enemies being vanquished, hath settled in Peace the Church of God, and this Holy See. And now, his Majesty having the Knowledge, Will, and Ability of composing This excel lent Book against this terrible Monster, has rendered himself no less admirable to the whole World, by the Eloquence of his Style, then by his great Wisdom. We render immortal Thanks to our Creator, who has raised up such a Prince, to defend His Church and this Holy See; most humbly beseeching Him bountifully to bestow on this Great Prince, a most happy Life, and all other good Things that he can wish for; and after his Exit from this transitory Life, to crown him in his celestial Kingdom, with a Crown of Eternal Glory. We, to our Power, by God s Assistance, shall not be wanting in the Performance of any Thing, that may tend to the Honor and Dignity of his Majesty, and to His and his Kingdom's Glory.

Leo, Bishop and Servant of the Servants of God To our most dear son in Christ, Henry, the illustrious King of England and Defender of the Faith

Greeting, and give his benediction.

By the good Pleasure and Will of Almighty God, presiding in the Government of the Universal Church, though unworthy so great Charge. We daily employ all our Thoughts, both at home and abroad, for the continual Propagation of the Holy Catholic Faith, without which none can be saved. And that the Methods which are taken for repressing of such as labor to overthrow the Church, or pervert, and stain her by wicked Glosses, and malicious Lies; may be carried on with continual Profit, as is ordered by the sound Doctrine of the Faithful, and especially of such as shine in the regal Dignity: We employ with all our Power, our Endeavors, and all the Parts of our Ministry.

And as the other Roman Bishops, our Predecessors, have been accustomed to bestow some particular Favors upon Catholic Princes, as the Exigencies of Affairs and Times required, especially on those who, in tempestuous Times, and whilst the rapid Perfidiousness of Schismatics and Heretics raged, not only persevered constantly in the true Faith, and unspotted Devotion of the holy Roman Catholic Church; but also as the Legitimate Sons and stoutest Champions of the same, have opposed themselves, both spiritually and temporally, against the mad Fury of Schismatics and Heretics: So also, We, for your Majesty s most excellent Works, and worthy Actions done for Us, and this Holy See, in which by divine Permission we preside; do desire to confer upon your Majesty, with Honor and immortal Praises, That, which may enable and engage you carefully to drive away from our Lord s Flock the Wolves; and cut off with the material Sword, the rotten Members that infect the mystical Body of Jesus Christ, and con firm the Hearts of the almost discomforted Faithful in the Solidity of Faith. Truly when our beloved Son John Clark, your Majesty's Orator, did lately in our Consistory, in presence of our venerable Brethren, Cardinals of the sacred Roman Church, and divers others holy Prelates; present unto Us, a Book, which Your Majesty, moved by your Charity, (which effects every Thing readily and well,) and enflamed with Zeal to the holy Catholic Faith, and Fervor of Devotion towards Us, and this Holy See; did compose, as a most noble and wholesome Antidote against the Errors of divers Heretics, often condemned by this Holy See, and now again revived by Martin Luther: When, I say, he offered this Book to Us, to be examined, and approved by Our Authority; and also declared, in a very eloquent Discourse, That, as Your Majesty, had by true Reasons, and the Undeniable Authority of Scripture, and holy Fathers, confuted the notorious Errors of Luther; so you are likewise ready, and resolved to prose cute, with all the Forces of your Kingdom, those who shall presume to follow, or defend them; having found in this Boole most admirable Doctrine, sprinkled with the Dew of Divine Grace; We rendered infinite Thanks to Almighty God, from whom every good Thing, and every perfect Gift proceeds, for being pleased to fill with his Grace, and to inspire your most excellent Mind, inclined to all Good, to defend, by your Writings, his Holy Faith, against the new Broacher of those condemned Errors; and to invite all other Christians, by your Example, to assist and favor, with all their Power, the orthodox Faith, and evangelical Truth, now under so great Peril and Danger.

Considering that it is but Just, that those, who under take pious Labors, in Defense of the Faith of Christ, should be extolled with all Praise and Honor; and being willing, not only to magnify with deserved Praise, and approve with our Authority, what your Majesty has with Learning and Eloquence writ against Luther; but also to Honor your Majesty with such a Title, as shall give all Christians to understand, as well in our times, as in succeeding Ages, how acceptable and welcome Your Gift was to Us, especially in this Juncture of Time: We, the true Successor of St. Peter, (whom Christ, before his Ascension, left as his Vicar upon Earth, and to whom he committed the Care of his Flock) presiding in this Holy See, from whence all
Dignity and Titles have their Source; have with our Brethren maturely deliberated on these Things; and with one Consent unanimously decreed to bestow on your Majesty this Title, viz. Defender of the Faith. And, as we have by this Title honored you; we likewise command all Christians, that they name your Majesty by this Title; and that in their Writings to your Majesty, immediately after the Word KING, they add,
Defender of the Faith. Having thus weighed, and diligently considered your singular Mer its, we could not have invented a more congruous Name, nor more worthy Your Majesty, than this worthy and most excellent Title; which, as often as you hear, or read, you shall remember your own Merits and Virtues: Nor will you, by this Title, exalt yourself, or become proud, but, according to your accustomed Prudence, rather more humble in the Faith of Christ; and more strong and constant in your Devotion to this Holy See, by which you were exalted. And you shall rejoice in our Lord, who is the Giver of all good Things, for leaving such a perpetual and everlasting Monument of your Glory to Posterity, and shewing the Way to others, that if they also covet to be invested with such a Title, they may study to do such Actions, and to follow the Steps of your most excellent Majesty; Whom, with your Wife, Children, and all who shall spring from you, We bless with a bountiful and liberal Hand; in the Name of Him from whom the Power of Benediction is given to Us, and by whom Kings reign, and Princes govern; and in whose Hands are the Hearts of Kings:

Praying, and beseeching the most High, to confirm your Majesty in your most holy Purposes, and to augment your Devotion; and for your most excellent Deeds in Defense of his Holy Faith, to render your Majesty so illustrious and famous to the whole World, as that our Judgment in adorning you with so remarkable a Title, may not be thought vain, or light, by any Person whatsoever; and finally, after you have finished your course in this Life, that he may make you Partaker of his eternal Glory. It shall not be lawful for any Person whatsoever, to infringe, or by any rash Presumption to act contrary to This Letter of Subscribing, and Command. But, if any one shall presume to make such attempt; let him know, that he shall thereby incur the indignation of Almighty God, and of the holy Apostles, Peter and Paul.

Given at St. Peter's in Home, the fifth of the Ides of October; in the Year of our Lord's Incarnation 1521, and in the ninth Year of our Papacy.

Letter from Pope Leo to Henry VIII
respecting the "Defense of the Seven Sacraments"

An acknowledgment of the nook written by the king against Luther

Most dear Son in Christ, Health and Apostolic Benediction:

Some days ago, when the envoy of Your Serenity, our beloved Son, John Clark, Dean of the Chapel Eoyal, publicly in Consistory presented us the book which Your Serenity has published against the impious teachings and sect of Martin Luther, and in a brilliant address, exceedingly appropriate to the occasion, declared, in the presence of a number of Prelates of the Roman Court, your readiness to aid Us and the Holy See with sword and pen, our soul was filled with joy. Not We alone, but all Our venerable brethren rejoiced, as though deeming that Luther s impiety had, not without the divine permission, assailed the Church of Christ, so that to her greater glory she might be fortunate enough to find such a champion and defender.

Hence, we have resolved, and all agree in Our decision, that your exceptional virtue and piety should be made memorable by some mark of Our love and appreciation. For if it has often been, most dear Son, a source of honor to great monarchs to take up arms to safeguard the liberty and tranquility of the Holy Apostolic See, how much more glory and reverence should accrue from employing the weapons of the Spirit of God and of heavenly science to remove from the faith of Christ so great a stain, and to preserve inviolate those sacraments by which the salvation of souls is secured.

These two functions, which hitherto We have always found separate, have been united in you alone, a mighty sovereign, in a most eminent degree; for you have both vindicated the liberty of the Church with your arms, and you have evinced your desire to fortify the Christian faith against impious heresy by the treasures of your piety and learning. The one is an evidence of invincible and lofty courage, the other of a spirit and sense of religion tender, devout, and orthodox.

In what words, then, or by what manner of eulogy shall we praise this piety, this plenitude of doctrine, overflowing as though from a celestial fountain? What fit return can we make for your kindness in dedicating to us so noble a product of your intellect? Both considerations exceed the powers of language, or even of thought; nor can we reflect on your services and deserts without being overcome.

What love, what zeal is yours for the defense of Christian faith! What benevolence in Our regard! And in the book itself, what solidity of matter, clearness of method, force of eloquence, wherein the Holy Spirit Himself shows visibly! It is thoroughly judicious, wise, and pious; charitable in instruction, gentle in admonition, correct in argument. If there be any of your opponents who have not fallen entirely into the power of the Prince of Darkness, they must be drawn by your writings to a saner condition of mind, if any chance for sanity be left.

These are distinguished and admirable achievements; and as they have been wrought in a new fashion, by a princely favor, for Almighty God and the Holy See, we render you, "Defender of the Faith, unbounded thanks. The Apostolic See thanks you; all who worship Christ and unite in His faith thank you. We, for Our part, with the concurrence of Our venerable brothers, bestow on you, in other letters sealed with lead, as you will find from their perusal, this title of Defender of the Faith. For your part, most dear Son, however you may consider great and desirable these honors which the Holy Apostolic See grants you as a reward of eminent virtue and a mark of its grateful appreciation, realize that greater and more glorious compensation is prepared for you in heaven by Our Lord and Savior. In upholding His cause and His spouse by every means of defense you have displayed your spirit and your virtue; and while you review those titles which you have acquired on earth and in heaven, remember by what claims you have gained them. Show yourself hereafter such as you have been heretofore. Let your later deeds be equal to your sublime and glorious beginnings. Let the Apostolic See, once defended by your arms, and the Christian faith, now fortified by the shield of your doctrine against the criminal frenzy of heretics, find and prove you ever a helper in all their perils, so that this extraordinary and unspeakable glory which Your Majesty has most mightily merited by your great efforts may continue to the last day of your life and endure to all future time as a theme of eulogy.

Given at Rome, at St. Peter s, under the seal of the Fisherman, the fourth day of November, 1521, the ninth year of Our Pontificate.

Letter of Dedication

To our most Holy Father, Leo, chief Bishop of Rome

Henry, King of England, France, and Ireland, wishes of perpetual happiness

Most Holy Father:

Perhaps it may appear strange to Your Holiness, that Part of our Youth being spent in martial Affairs, and Part in the Studies of Things belonging to the Commonwealth; we should now undertake the Task of a Man, that ought to have employed all his Time in the Studies of Learning; in opposing Our self against this growing Heresy. But Your Holiness (I suppose) will the less admire, when You consider the Reasons that obliged Us to take upon Us this Charge of Writing. We have seen Tares cast into our Lord's Harvest[1]; Sects do spring up, and Heresies increase so much as almost, to overthrow the Faith of Christ: And such Seeds of Discord are sown abroad in the World, that no sincere Christian, can suffer, or endure any longer their spreading Mischiefs, without an Obligation of employing all his Studies and Forces to oppose them. Your Holiness ought not therefore to wonder, if We (not the greatest in Ability, yet in Faith and Good- will inferior to none,) have proposed to Our self, to employ our Force and Power in a Work so necessary, and so profitable, that it cannot lightly be omitted by any, without Offence; also to declare Our great Respect towards Your Holiness, Our Endeavors for the Propagation of the Faith of Christ, and Our Obedience to the Service of Almighty God: Greatly confiding, that although our Learning is not much, nay in Comparison, even Nothing; yet His Grace will so co-operate with Us, that what we are not able thereby to effect, He, by his Benignity and Power, may more fully perform, and by his Strength supply Our Weakness therein. Though we know very well, that there are every-where several more expert, especially in Holy Writ, who could have more commodiously undertaken this Great Work, and performed it much better than We: Yet are We not altogether so ignorant, as not to esteem it Our Duty, to employ, with all Our Might, Our Wit and Pen in the common Cause. For having, by long Experience, found, that Religion bears the greatest Sway in the Administration of Public Affairs, and is likewise of no small Importance in the Commonwealth; We have employed no little Time, especially since We came to Years of Discretion, in the Contemplation thereof; wherein We have always taken great Delight: And though not ignorant of Our small Progress therein made; yet, at least, it is so much, as, We hope, (especially with the Help, or rather Instigation of such Things as can instruct the most Ignorant, viz. Piety, and the Grief of seeing Religion abused,) will suffice for Reasons to discover the Subtilties of Luther's Heresy. We have therefore, (confiding in those Things,) entered upon this Work; dedicating to Your Holiness what We have meditated therein; that, under Your Protection, who are Christ s Vicar upon Earth, it may pass the public Censure. For we are persuaded that this Heresy, having for some Time exercised its Rage amongst Christians; and being by

---

[1] Matt. 13:25

Your most weighty and wholesome Sentence condemned, and, as it were, by Force plucked out of Men's Hands, if any Thing remains hidden in the Bowels of it, fed by Flattery and fair Promises; it is to be rooted out by just Reasons, and Arguments; that, as Men's Wits suffer themselves, more willingly to be led than drawn; so Reason also may supply these with the mildest Remedies. Whether or not any Thing is effectually done in this, shall rest to Your Holiness s Judgment: If We have erred in any Thing, we offer it to be corrected as may please Your Holiness.

To the Reader

Although I do not rank myself amongst the most Learned and Eloquent; yet (shunning the Stain of ingratitude, and moved by Fidelity and Piety;) I cannot but think myself obliged, (would to God my Ability to do it, were equal to my good Will!) to defend my Mother, the Spouse of Christ: Which, though it be a Subject more copiously handled by others ; nevertheless I account it as much my own Duty, as his who is the most learned, by my utmost Endeavors, to defend the Church, and to oppose myself to the poisonous Shafts of the Enemy that fights against her: Which this Juncture of Time, and the present State of Things, require at my Hand. For before, when none did assault, it was not necessary to resist; but now when the Enemy, (and the most wicked Enemy imaginable,) is risen up, who, by the Instigation of the Devil, under Pretext of Charity, and stimulated by Anger and Hatred, spews out the Poison of Vipers against the Church, and Catholic Faith; it is necessary that every Servant of Christ, of what Age, Sex, or Order so-ever, should rise against this
common Enemy of the Christian Faith; that those, whose Power avails not, yet may testify their good Will by their cheerful Endeavors.

It is now therefore convenient, that we arm ourselves with a two-fold Armor: the one Celestial, and the other Terrestrial. With a celestial Armor; That he, who, by a feigned and dissembled Charity, destroys others, and perishes himself, being gained by true Charity, may also gain others; and that he who fights by a false doctrine, may be conquered by true Doctrine: With a terrestrial; that, if he be so obstinately malicious, as to neglect holy Councils, and despise God's Reproofs, he may be constrained by due Punishments; that he who will not do Good, may leave off doing Mischief[2]; and he that did Harm by the Word of Malice, may do Good by the Example, of his Punishments. What Plague so pernicious did ever invade the Flock of Christ? What Serpent so venomous has crept in, as he who writ of the Babylonian Captivity of the Church; who wrests Holy Scripture by his own Sense, against the Sacraments of Christ; abolishes the ecclesiastical Rites and Ceremonies left by the Fathers; undervalues the holy and ancient Interpreters of Scripture, unless they concur with his Sentiments; calls the most Holy See of Rome, Babylon, and the Pope's Authority, Tyranny; esteems the most wholesome Decrees of the Universal Church to be Captivity; and turns the Name of the most Holy Bishop of Rome, to that of Antichrist? O that detest able Trumpeter of Pride, Calumnies, and Schisms! What an infernal Wolf is he, who seeks to disperse the Flock of Christ?[3] What a great Member of the Devil is he,): who endeavors to tear the Christian Members of Christ from their Head?

How infectious is his Soul, who revives these detest able Opinions and buried Schisms; adds new ones to the old, brings to Light (Cerberus-like, from Hell) the
Heresies which ought to lie in eternal Darkness; and esteems himself worthy to govern all Things by his own Word, opposed against the Judgments of all the
Ancients; nay also to ruin the Church of God! Of whose Malice I know not what to say. For I think neither Tongue nor Pen can express the Greatness of it. Wherefore,

---

[2] Rom. 13:3-4)
[3] Matt. 7:15

before I exhort, pray, and beseech, through the Name of Christ (which we will profess) all Christians, who are willing to look upon, and read Luther's Works, especially the Babylonian Captivity, (if he be Author of it) to do it warily, and very judicially; that, as Virgil said, lie gathered Gold out of the Dross of Ennius; so they may also gather good Things out of Evil: And if anything please them, let them not be so taken with it, as to suck the Poison with the Honey; for it is better to want both, than to swallow both. To hinder which, I wish the Author may Repent, be converted, and live[4]; and, in Imitation of St. Augustine, (whose Rule he professed) correct his Books, filled with Malice, and revoke his Errors. If Luther refuses this, it will shortly come to pass, if Christian Princes do their Duty, that these Errors, and himself, if he perseveres therein, may be burned in the Fire. In the meanwhile, we thought it fit to discover to the Readers some chief Heads or Chapters in the Babylonian Captivity, which have the most Venom in them, by which it will appear, very clearly, with what exulcerated Mind he began this Work; pretending the public Good, but writing Nothing but malicious Inventions.

We need not seek any foreign Testimonies for proving what we have said; for Luther (fearing that any one should go up and down in Search of such,) discovers himself, and his Mind, of his own Accord, in his very Beginning. For who should doubt of what he aimed at, when he reads this one Sentence of his?

---

[4] Ezek. 33:11

CHAPTER I
Indulgences and the Pope's Authority
(Indulgeniice suni adulaiorum Romanorum nequitice)

As every living Creature is known chiefly by its Face, so by this first Proposition it evidently appears, how corrupt and rotten his Heart was, whose Mouth, being filled with Bitterness, broke out into such a Corruption; for what he said of Indulgences in times past, seemed to many, not only to detract much of the Roman Bishop's Power, but also to lessen the good Hope and holy Consolation of the Faithful, and mightily to excite Men to confide in the Riches of their own Penitence, and despise the Treasures of the Holy Church, and the Bounty of God: And yet what he then writ, was favorably interpreted, because he only disputed many of them, but did not affirm them; desiring to be taught, and promising to obey him that would instruct him better. But what this new Saint, (who refers all things to the Holy Spirit, which cannot brook anything of Falsehood,) did then write with a simple intention, is easily discovered: For as soon as he had any Thing of wholesome Advice given him, he immediately vomited his Malediction against those, who endeavored his Good, reviling them with Reproaches and quarrels; for which it is worth our While to see what height of Folly he is come to at last. He confessed before that Indulgences were good, at least to absolve us, besides the Crime, from the Punishments also which should be enjoined us by the Order of the Church, or.by our particular Priest: But now it was not by Learning, (as he says himself,) but by mere Malice that he wrought; and, contradicting himself, he condemns Indulgences; and says, That they are nothing but mere Impostures, fit only to destroy People s Money, and God's Faith. Every Man may see how wickedly and furiously he rails in this Matter: For, if Indulgences, as he says, are but mere Impostures, and good for Nothing, then it follows, that not only our Chief Bishop, Leo X. (whose innocent, unspotted Life, and most holy Conversation are well known through the World, as Luther himself confesses in a Letter of his to the Pope) is an Impostor; but also all Roman Bishops in so many past ages, are so, w r ho, as Luther himself says, did use to give Indulgences; some a Year's Remission; some three years; some to forgive a Lent's Penance; some a certain part of the whole Penance, as the Third, or one Half; at least something., as to plenary, or full Remission of the Sin and Punishment.

Then were they all Impostors, if Luther be true: But how much more Reason is there to believe, that this little Brother is a scabbed Sheep, than that so many pastors were treacherous, and unfaithful? For Luther, as is said above, shews what Kind of Man he is, and how uncharitable, when he blushes not, to lay such a crime against so great, and so holy Bishops. If God (in Leviticus) says to all, thou shalt not be an Accuser, or Backbiter amongst the People[5]; what may we think of Luther, who casts such a foul Scandal, not only on one Man, but on so many, and so venerable Prelates? And this he whispers, not only in one City, but publishes to the whole World. If he be accursed (as in Deuteronomy) who shall privately smite his Neighbor;[6] with how great a Curse shall he be struck, who insults over his Governors with such Reproaches? Finally,[7] (as the Gospel says) lie be a Murderer, and has not Life everlasting, who hates his Brother[8]; does not this Parricide deserve everlasting Death, who, with hatred pursues his Father? Seeing he is come to that pass, as to deny Indulgences to be profitable in this life; it would be in vain for me to dispute what great benefits the Souls in Purgatory receive by them: Moreover, what would it avail us to discourse with him of the great Helps, whereby we are relieved from Purgatory itself? Not able to endure to hear of the Pope s delivering any Person out of it, he presumes to leave none there himself.

What Profit is there to dispute, or fight against him, who fights against himself? What should my Arguments avail me, though I force him to confess what he before denied, since he now denies what before he confessed? But admit the Pope's Indulgences were disputable; yet it is necessary that the Words of Christ remain firm, by which he gave the Keys of the Church to St. Peter, when he said, whatsoever thou shalt bind on Earth, shall be bound in Heaven; and whatsoever thou shalt loose on Earth, shall be loosed in Heaven: Likewise, Whose Sins ye forgive, shall be forgiven unto them, and whosoever Sins ye retain, shall be retained. By which Words, if it is manifest that any Priest has power to absolve Men from Sins, and take away eternal punishment due there unto; who will not judge it ridiculous, that the Prince of all Priests should be denied the taking away of temporal Punishment?

But perhaps some may say, that Luther will not admit that any Priest has Power of binding, or loosing any Thing; or that the Chief Bishop has any greater power than other Bishops or Priests: But what concerns it me, what that Man admits, or denies, who granted many Things a while ago, which now he denies, and who, alone, rejects all Things which the Holy Church has held during so many Ages? For (to omit other Things which this new Momus, or feigned Deity censures) certainly if the Popes have erred, who granted Indulgences; the whole Congregation of the Faithful were not free from Sin, who received them for so long a Time, and with so great Content: In whose Judgment, and in the Custom observed by the Saints, I doubt not but we may rather acquiesce, than in Luther alone, who furiously condemns the whole Church, whose Chief Bishops, he not only loads with mad Reproaches, but also fears not to publish, that this Supremacy of the Pope is but a vain Name, and is effectually Nothing but the

---

[5] Lev. 19:16
[6] Deut. 27:24
[7] Matt. 16:19, John 20:22
[8] I John 3:15

Kingdom of Babylon, and the Power of Nimrod, that strong Hunter; and desires his Readers, and the Book-binders, that (burning whatsoever he first writ of Papacy,) they may reserve this one Proposition.

CHAPTER II
On the Pope's authority
(Papatus est robusta Venatio Romani Pontificis)

Indeed, it is no ridiculous Desire in him, to wish the things he writ before should be burned; because many of them deserved it; yet much more this Proposition, which he desires may be preserved after the rest are burned, as if worthy of Eternity. What Man, if he had not known his Malice, but would have admired his in constancy in this Place? For first, he denied the Pope's Supremacy to be of divine Right, or Law, but allowed it to be of human Right: But now, (contrary to himself) he affirms it to be of neither of them; but that the Papacy, by mere Force has assumed, and usurped Tyranny. Formerly he was of Opinion, That Power was given to Roman Bishops over the Universal Church by human Consent, and for the public Good: And so much was he of that Opinion, that he detested the Schism of the Bohemians, who denied any Obedience to the See of Rome; saying, That they sinned damnably who did not obey the Pope: Having written these Things so little Time before, he now embraces what then he detested. The like Stability he has in this: That after he preached, in a Sermon to the People, That Excommunication is a Medicine, and to be suffered with Patience and Obedience; he himself, being (for every good Cause,) a while after excommunicated, was so im patient of that Sentence, that (mad with Rage) he breaks forth into insupportable Contumelies, Reproaches and Blasphemies: So that by his Fury, it plainly appears, that those who are driven from the Bosom of their Holy Mother the Church, are immediately seized, and possessed with Furies, and tormented by Devils. But I ask this; he that saw these Things so short a while since, how is it that he becomes of Opinion, that then he saw Nothing at all? What new Eyes has he got? Is his Sight more sharp, after he has joined Anger to his wonted Pride, and has added Hatred to both? Does he see farther with these so excellent Spectacles?

I will not wrong the Bishop of Rome so much, as troublesomely, or carefully to dispute his Right, as if it were a Matter doubtful; it is sufficient for my present Task, that the

Enemy is so much led by Fury, that he destroys his own Credit, and makes clearly appear, that by mere Malice he is so blinded, that he neither sees, nor knows what he says himself. For he cannot deny, but that all the Faithful honor and acknowledge the sacred Roman See for their Mother and Supreme, nor does Distance of Place or Dangers in the Way hinder Access thereunto. For if those who come hither from the Indies tell us Truth, the Indians themselves (separated from us by such a vast Distance, both of Land and Sea,) do submit to the See of Rome. If the Bishop of Rome has got this large Power, neither by Command of God, nor the Will of Man, but by main Force: I would fain know of Luther, when the Pope rushed into the Possession of so great Riches? for so vast a Power, (especially if it begun in the Memory of Man,) cannot have an obscure Origin. But perhaps he will say, it is above one or two Ages since; let him then point out the Time by Histories: Otherwise, if it be so ancient that the Beginning of so great a Thing is quite forgot; let him know, that, by all Laws, we are forbidden to think otherwise, then that Thing had a lawful Beginning, which so far surpasses the Memory of Man, that its Origin cannot be known. It is certain, that, by the unanimous Consent of all Nations, it is forbidden to change, or move the Things which have been for a long Time immoveable. Truly, if any will look upon ancient Monuments, or read the Histories of former Times, he may easily find, that since the Conversion of the World, all Churches in the Christian World have been obedient to the See of Borne. We find, that, though the Empire was translated to the Grecians, yet did they still own, and obey the Supremacy of the Church, and See of Rome, except when they were in any turbulent Schism.

St. Jerome excellently well demonstrates his good Esteem for the Roman See, when he openly declares, (though he was no Roman himself) that it was sufficient for him, that the Pope of Rome did but approve his Faith, whoever else should disapprove it.

When Luther so impudently asserts, (and that against his former Sentence,) That the Pope has no Kind of Right over the Catholic Church; no, not so much as human; but has by mere Force tyrannically usurped it; I cannot but admire, that he should expect his Readers should be so easily induced to believe his Words; or so blockish, as to think that a Priest, without any Weapon, or Company to defend him, (as doubtless he was, before he enjoyed that which Luther says he usurped,) could ever expect or hope, without any Right or Title, to obtain so great a Command over so many Bishops, his Fellows, in so many different, and divers Nations. How could he expect, I say, that any Body would believe, (as I know not how he could desire they should,) that all Nations, Cities, nay Kingdoms and Provinces, should be so prodigal of their Rights and Liberties, as to acknowledge the Superiority of a strange Priest, to whom they should owe no Subjection? But what signifies it to know the Opinion of Luther in this Case, when (through Anger and Malice,) he himself is ignorant of his own Opinion, or what he thinks? But he manifestly discovers the Darkness of his Understanding and Knowledge, and the Folly and Blindness of his Heart, abandoned to a reprobate Sense, in doing and saying Things so inconsistent. How true is that saying of the Apostle? Though I have Prophecy, and understand all Mysteries, and all Knowledge; and though I have all Faith, so as to remove Mountains, and have not

Charity, I am Nothing.[9] Of which Charity Luther not only shews how void he is, by perishing himself through Fury; but much more by endeavoring to draw all others with him into Destruction, whilst he strives to dissuade them from their Obedience to the Chief Bishop, whom, in a three-fold Manner, he himself is bound to obey, viz. as a Christian, as a Priest, and as a religious Brother; his Disobedience also deserving to be punished in a treble Manner: He remembers not how much Obedience is better than Sacrifice, if not does he consider how it is ordained in Deuteronomy, That the Man that will do presumptuously, and will not hearken unto the Priest, (that stands to minister there before the Lord thy God,) or unto the Judge, even that Man shall die: He considers not, I say, what cruel Punishment he deserves, that will not obey the chief Priest and supreme Judge upon Earth. For this poor Brother, being cited to appear before the Pope, with Offers to pay his Expenses, and Promise of safe Conduct; he refuses to go without a Guard; troubling the whole Church as much as he could, and exciting the whole Body to rebel against the Head; which to do, is as the Sin of Witchcraft; and in whom to acquiesce, is as the Sin of Idolatry[10] Seeing therefore that Luther, (moved by Hatred) runs head-long on to Destruction, and refuses to submit to the Law of God, but desires to establish a Law of his own; it behoves all Christians to beware, lest (as the Apostle says) through the Disobedience of one, many be made Sinners; but on the contrary, by hating and detesting his Wickedness, we may sing with the Prophet, I hated the wicked, and loved your Law.

---

[9] 1 Corn. 13:2, 1 Ki. 15:22, Deut. 17:12
[10] 1 Ki. 15:23, Rom. 5:19, Ps. 118, 113

CHAPTER Ill
The Defense of the Seven Sacraments

But these two Chapters, (of abrogating Indulgences, and taking away all Authority of the chief Bishop,) of which we have already given our Opinion; though they are wicked, yet are they but the Flourishings or first Essays of Luther, who now begins to murder and destroy the Sacraments, which in his Book he goes about to do; all which whole Book, he confesses to be but a Flourish, to I know not what Work: I suppose it is some Work, in which he intends to fight more seriously against our most holy Faith, yet I much admire he should think to compose any Thing whatsoever, more stuffed with Venom, then is this whole Preface, or Flourish of his: In which of seven Sacraments, he leaves us but three, nor them neither, unless for a Time; giving us to understand, that he shall soon also take them from us; for of the three, he takes away one immediately after in the same Book; whereby he plainly shews us what he intends to do with the rest.

To which Undertaking it seems he prepares the Way, when he says, that if he would speak according to Scripture, he would leave but one Sacrament and three Sacramental Signs. If anyone does but diligently examine how he handles these three Sacraments, (which, for the present, he puts as three Sacraments, or under three Signs) he may perceive that he treats of them in such a Manner, as that none should doubt, but that when he sees his own Time, and at his own Pleasure, he intends wholly to deprive us of them all. Let the Reader diligently observe his Steps, and look to his own, that he may discover the Subtilties of this Serpent; and let him not, with too much Security, thrust himself amongst these Thorns, Brambles, and Dens, but warily walk round his Caverns, fearing lest he should secretly strike his mortal Sting into his Heel: This hideous Monster being caught, will become be numbed, and pine away by his own Venom.

CHAPTER IV
Sacrament of the altar

Let us therefore begin where he began himself, with the adorable Sacrament of Christ's Body. The changing of the Name thereof, calling it, The Sacrament of Bread, shews that this Man cannot well endure, that we should be put in Mind of Christ s Body, by the Name of the Blessed Sacrament; and that, if under any fair Pretext, it was possible for him, he would give it a worse Name. How much differs the Judgment of St. Ambrose from this Man's, when he says, Though the Form of the
Bread and Wine is seen upon the Altar, yet we must believe, that there is Nothing else but the Body and Blood of Christ: By which Words it clearly appears, that St. Ambrose confesses no other Substance to remain with the Body and Blood of Christ in the Sacrament, when he says, that which is seen under the Form of Bread and Wine, is Nothing else but the Body and Blood of Christ. If St. Ambrose had only said Flesh and Blood, without adding any Thing more, perhaps Luther would have said, that the Bread and Wine were there also; as Luther himself says, That the Substance of the Flesh is with the Bread, and the Substance of the Blood along with the Wine: But seeing St. Ambrose says, that there is Nothing else but the Flesh and Blood, it appears that he is manifestly against Luther, who affirms, That the Bread is with the Flesh, and the Wine with the Blood.

And though this which Luther says, were as true as it is false, viz. That the Bread should remain mingled with the Body of Christ; yet was it not necessary for him to blot the Name of the Body of Christ out of the Sacrament, in which he confesses that the true Body of Christ is. For if the Substance of Bread should be with the Body of Christ, (as he contends,) yet there is no Reason that the inferior Substance should take away the Name from the more worthy: Because, though the Apostle, (conforming himself to the Understanding of the Auditors, then ignorant People,) called it Bread; yet now, after the Faith has been so long established, it was not fit or convenient to change this so adorable a Name, (which represents to the Hearers, the Thing in the Sacrament,) into such a Name as would have turned their Minds from the Body to the Bread; neither would Luther, without Doubt, have changed it, if he had not determined with himself to draw the People to worship the Bread, and leave out Christ's Body; from which he himself is divided; concerning which, I shall presently speak more fully.

In the meanwhile, let us truly examine how subtlety, under Pretense of favoring the Laity, he endeavors to stir them up to an Hatred against the Clergy: For when he resolved to render the Church's Faith suspicious, that its Authority should be of no Consequence against him; (and so, by opening that Gap, he might destroy the chiefest Mysteries of Christianity,) he began with that Thing, which he foresaw would be praised and applauded by the People: For he touched the old Sore, by which Bohemia had been formerly blistered, viz. That the Laity ought to receive the Eucharist under both Kinds. When first he began to handle this Point, he only said, That the Pope would do well, to have it ordained by a general Council, that the Laity should receive the Sacrament under both Kinds; but that being by some disputed with him, and denied, he contented not himself to stop there, but grew to such a perverse Height, that he condemned the whole Clergy of Wickedness, for not doing it without staying for any Council. For my Part, I do not dispute the first: And though to me, no Reason appear why the Church should not ordain, that the Sacrament should be administered to the Laity, under both Kinds; yet doubt I not, but what was done in Times past, in omitting it, and also in hindering it to be so administered now, is very convenient. Nor can I believe the whole Clergy, (during so many ages) to have been so void of Sense, as to incur eternal Punishment for a Thing by which they could reap no temporal Good. It further appears not to be a Thing of any such Danger; because God, not only bestowed Heaven upon those Men, who did this Thing themselves and writ that it ought to be done; but likewise, would have them honored on Earth, by those by whom he is adored himself: Amongst whom (to omit others,) was that most learned and holy Man Thomas Aquinas, whom I the more willingly name here; because the Wickedness of Luther cannot endure the Sanctity of this Man, but reviles with his foul Lips, him whom all Christians honor. There are very many, though not canonized, who are contrary to Luther s Opinion in this; and to whom, in Piety and Learning, Luther is in no wise comparable:

Among whom are the Master of the Sentences, Nicholas de Lyra, and many others; to each of whom it behoves all Christians to give more Credit, than to Luther. But pray observe how Luther staggers, and contradicts himself: In one Place, he says, That Christ, in his last Supper, not only said to all the Faithful, as permitting, but as commanding, Drink ye all of this:[11] Yet afterwards, (fearing to offend the Laity, whom he flatters, with a View to stir up their Hatred against the Priests,) he adds these Words, not that they, who use but one Kind do sin against Christ, seeing Christ did not command to use any Kind, but left it to every Man's Discretion, saying, as often as ye do this, do it in Remembrance of me: But, says he, they sin who forbid to give both Kinds to such as are willing to receive them: The Blame, says he, lies on the Clergy, and not on the Laity. You see how clearly, he first holds it for a Command, and then says, it is no Commandment, but a Thing left to every Man's Discretion. What need we contradict him, who so often contradicts himself?

---

[11] Matt. 26:27

And yet before, when he speaks of all, in general, he does not defend the Laity well, if any Body would urge the Matter: And he proves no Sin to be in the Priests, whom he accuses most bitterly: For, he says, the Sin consists in the Priest s taking the Liberty of one Kind from the Laity: If any Body should ask him here, how he knows that Custom to have been practiced against the People's Will? I believe he cannot tell it. Why then does he condemn the whole Clergy, for having taken the Laity's Right from them by Force, seeing he cannot by any Testimony prove that this was forcibly done? How much more reasonable should it be, to say, that the Con sent of the People did concur with this Custom for so many Ages, if it could not be justly established but with their Pleasure? For my Part, when I see what Things the Clergy cannot obtain from the Laity, (not even an Exemption from burying their Dead almost under their Altars) I cannot easily believe that they should suffer themselves to be injuriously, and by Force, deprived of any such great Part of their Rights; but that rather this was instituted for some reasonable Causes, and with the Consent of the Laity.

What I most admire, is, that Luther should be so angry and passionate, for having one Kind taken away from the Laity in the Communion; but is Nothing at all moved that Children should be debarred from both: For he cannot deny, but that Children, in the primitive Times, did receive the Communion: Which Custom, if it was justly omitted, (though Christ said, Drink ye all of this[12]) and that, without Doubt, for very good Reasons, (though no Body can now remember them) why should we not think that it was for good and just Reasons, unknown at this Time, the primitive Custom of the Laity s receiving the Sacrament in both Kinds, (which perhaps continued not for any considerable Time,) was taken away?

Moreover, if he examines the strict Form of the Evangelical Narration, and leaves Nothing in this Matter to the Church; why does he not command the Sacrament to be always received at Supper-time, or rather after it?

Finally, it should not be esteemed less inconvenient to do any Thing in the Manner of receiving this Sacrament, which ought not to be done. If therefore the Custom of the whole Church does not well, in denying to the Laity the Communion under the Form of Wine, by what Reason durst Luther put Water into the Wine? For I do not think that he is so bold as to consecrate without Water; yet has he no Example in our Lord's Supper, nor any certain one, of the Apostles Tradition, of mingling the Wine with Water: But he learned it only by the Custom of the Church; to which, if he thinks himself obliged to be obedient in this Part, why does he so arrogantly oppose it in the other?

Whatever Luther chatters concerning this Matter; for my Part I judge it more safe, to believe that the Laity do rightly communicate, though under one Kind; than that the Clergy, for so many Ages, were damned, for omitting both, (as he disputes;) for he calls them all wicked, and so wicked, that they all were guilty of the Crime of Evangelical Treason, (says he) we must name them that are Heretics and Schismatic; it is not the Bohemians, or Grecians, (for they endeavor to follow the Gospel) but the Romans who

---

[12] Matt. 26:27

are the Heretics and Schismatics, and, by their Fictions, presume against the evident Truth of Scripture.

If Luther admits Nothing else, but the evident and plain Text of Scripture, why does he not (as I said) command the Eucharist to be received at Supper-time? For the Scriptures mention that Christ did so. How much better should Luther believe, that this Institution of the Church, in giving the Communion to the Laity under one Kind, was done by the Authority of God, not by any human Invention, as it was by God s Authority instituted that it should be received when the People are fasting: For as St. Augustin says, it has pleased the Holy Ghost, that the Body of our Lord, which, by the Apostles, was received after other Meats, should, in the Church, be received fasting, before any other Meats? It is very probable, that the Holy Ghost, which governs the Church of Christ, as he has changed the Time of receiving the Sacrament, from Supper, to the Morning,
fasting, has also changed the Laity's receiving under both, to the communicating under one Kind: For he that could change the one, why could he not also alter the other.

Luther shews plainly in this Place, that his Intention is to flatter the Bohemians, whose Perfidiousness he before detested: For none of those, whom he calls Papists, and Flatterers of the Pope, do so much flatter the Roman Prelates, as Luther flatters the very Scum of the Bohemian Commonalty; and not without Reason indeed; for he foresees that the Germans, (whom he formerly deceived under the Form of a simple Sheep,) would reject him, as soon as they should perceive him to be a devouring Wolf. And therefore, he insinuates himself into the Esteem of the Bohemians, and makes him self-Friends of the Mammon of Iniquity[13] (as much as he is able,) that when he is banished his own Country, he may pass into that of those, into whose Errors he has already entered.

And that some remarkable Action may render him more commendable to them when he goes, he endeavors to extinguish all the Force and Authority of Ecclesiastical Customs, and so, in the Conclusion, to ruin all, if his Designs should take; which God forbid!

He aims at greater Things than he can expect to accomplish; and therefore, pleads for the Laity, though his Thoughts are quite contrary to what he pretends; for though he sweetly offers them Bread in the one Hand, yet he holds a Scourge for them in the other. In the first Place, he is altogether for the Laity's being admitted to receive under both Kinds: (And who would not think, that he thereby endeavors to increase their Devotion towards the Sacrament[14]) But look a little further what he drives at: For at last he brings his Business so far, as to desire, that they may not be obliged to receive at Easter; and that no Time maybe appointed them for receiving, but that every Man may be left to his own Discretion; nay further, that none should receive more than once, in his whole Life, and that at the Day of his Death; which is uncertain, and at which many are not able to receive. So, he that pretended to stand for the

---

[13] Lu. 16:9
[14] Lu. 9:11

communicating under both Kinds, recommends the quite Contrary, to wit, that it may be lawful for them never to receive under any Kind; and he esteems it an excel lent Liberty, that the People may be altogether freed from receiving the Sacrament at all.

Wherefore, though this Serpent seems to flatter you with an amiable Aspect; yet that venomous Tail of his seeks to sting you: For he makes it plainly appear, that he is more concerned for the People s receiving under one Kind, then for their abstaining from both. And even as the old Serpent, being cast out of Heaven, envied Man's Happiness in Paradise; so Luther, being fallen, by his own Sin, under the Penalty of Excommunication, (and thereby deprived of the wholesome and life-giving Communion under both Kinds,) endeavors to entrap all others in the same Snare; in Order, that, being freed from the Obligation of receiving under both Kinds, they may, by little and little, bring themselves under no Kind at all. And the further you advance in reading his Libel, the more you will discover this detestable Fetch of his.

He makes it a second Captivity, that any Man should be forbidden to believe, that the true Bread and true Wine remain after Consecration: So that in this, (contrary to the Belief of the whole Christian World, both now, and for so many Ages past,) he endeavors to persuade, that the Body and Blood of Christ are after such a Manner in the Eucharist, that the Substance of true Bread and true Wine remains still after Consecration. I suppose, afterwards, when it pleases him, he will deny the Substance of the Body and Blood to be there, when he has a Mind to change his Opinion, as he has three Times done already; and yet he feigns that he teaches those Things, as being moved with Pity towards the Captivity of the Israelites, in which they are kept Slaves to Babylon. Thus, he calls the whole Church, Babylon, and the Faith of Christ, Slavery: And this merciful Man offers Liberty to all those, who will divide themselves from the Church, and become corrupted with the Infection of this rotten and separated Member: But it is worth our While to know by what Means he invites People to this more than servile Liberty.

He esteems this to be his greatest and chiefest Reason, to wit, That Scripture is not to be forced, either by Men or Angels; but to be kept in the simplest Signification that can be: And (says he) unless for some manifest Circumstances requiring, it is not to be taken otherwise than in its proper and grammatical Sense; lest Occasion should be given to the Adversaries to under value the whole Scriptures: But (says he) the Divine Words are forced, if that which Christ called Bread, be taken for the Accidents of Bread; and what he called Wine, for the Form of Wine: Therefore, by all Means, the true Bread and true Wine remain upon the Altar, lest Violence be done to Christ s Words, if the Species be taken for the Substance. For, (says he) seeing that the Evangelists so plainly write, that Christ took Bread, and blessed it; and, afterwards, in the Book of the Acts, and by Paul, it is called Bread, we ought to take it for true Bread, and true Wine, as a true Chalice. For they do not say themselves, that the Chalice is transubstantiated.

This is Luther s great, and (as he says) his chief Reason; which I hope so to handle, as to give all Men to understand, of how little Consequence it is. For in the first Place, though the Evangelists had plainly said, what he says they did; yet that does not prove any Thing clearly for him; but on the Contrary, they say nothing in any Place that may seem to favor his Side. Do not they write (says he) that he took Bread, and blessed it? And what does that argue? We confess he took Bread, and blessed it; But that he gave Bread to his Disciples, after he had made it his Body, we flatly deny; and the Evangelists do not say he did: That this may more evidently appear, and that there may be less Room left for Wrangling; let us hear the Evangelists themselves:

St. Mathew's Words are these, while they were at Supper, Jesus took Bread and blessed it, and brake it, and gave it to his Disciples, saying, take, and eat, this is my Body: And taking the Chalice, he gave Thanks, and gave it to them, saying, drink ye all of this; This is my Blood of the New Testament, which is shed for many, for the Remission of Sins.* But St. Mark's Words are these, and while they were eating, Jesus took Bread, and blessed and brake it, and gave to them, and said, take, eat, this is my Body: And when he had taken the Chalice, and given Thanks, he gave it to them; and they all drank of it: And he said unto them, this is my Blood of the new Testament which is shed for many. St. Luke has it after this Manner, and he took Bread, and gave Thanks, and brake it, and gave unto them, saying, this is my Body which is given for you: This do in Remembrance of me; likewise, also the Chalice, after Supper, saying, This Chalice is the New Testament of my Blood, which is shed for you.[15]

In all these Words of the Evangelists, I see none, where, after the Consecration, the Sacrament is called Bread and Wine; but only Body and Blood. They say, That Christ took Bread in his Hands., which we all confess; but when the Apostles received it, it was not called Bread, but Body. Yet Luther endeavors to rest the Words of the Gospel, by his own Interpretation. Take, eat; this, that is, this Bread, (says he, which he had taken and broken,) is my Body. This is Luther s Interpretation; not Christ's Words, nor the Sense of his Words. If he had given to his Disciples, the Bread which he took, as he took it; without converting it into Flesh, before he bad them (in giving it) take and eat; it had been rightly said, that he gave what he took in his Hands; for then he had given Nothing else: But seeing he turned the Bread into his Flesh, before he gave it the Apostles to eat; they now receive, not the Bread which he took, but his Body, into which he had turned the Bread; as if one who had taken Seed, should give to another the Flower sprung thereof: He would not give what he had taken, though the common Course of Nature had made the one of the other. So likewise, much less did Christ give the Apostles what he took in his Hand, when, by so great a Miracle, he turned the Bread which he took, into his own Body; unless, perhaps, some will say, because Aaron took a Rod in his Hand, and cast a Rod from him[16], that the Substance of the Rod remained with the Serpent, and the Serpent's Substance with the Rod, when it was restored again: If the Rod could not remain with the Serpent, how much less can the Bread remain with the Flesh of Christ, that incomparable Substance?

As for what Luther argues, or rather trifles, to shew the Simplicity of his own Faith; when of the Wine, Christ does not say, Hoc, est Sanguis meus, but, Hie, est Sanguis meus: I wonder why it should enter into any Man's Mind to write thus: For who sees

---

[15] Lu. 22:19-20
[16] Ex. 7:12

not that this makes Nothing at all for him, nay, rather, does it not make against him? It had seemed more for his Purpose, if Christ had said, Hoc est Sanguis meus: For then he might have had some Color at least, whereby he might have referred the Article of Demonstrating to the Wine. But now, though Wine is of the neuter Gender; yet Christ did not say Hoc, but Hie est Sanguis meus. And though Bread is of the masculine Gender, yet, notwithstanding, he says, Hoc est Corpus meum, not Hie; that it may appear, by both Articles, that he did not mean to give either Bread or Wine, but his own Body and Blood. Is it not very ridiculous, that Luther should imagine this Pronoun Hoc, not to be by Christ's Intention referred to the Body, but only for the Convenience of the Greek and Latin Tongues; and therefore, sends us back to the Hebrew? For the Hebrew, if it has not the neuter Gender, cannot so conveniently declare to what Christ has referred this Article, as the Greek or Latin can do.

For though in the Hebrew, the Article should be of the masculine Gender, that is, Hie est Corpus meum; nevertheless, the Matter would be left doubtful, because that Speech might seem forced by the Necessity of the Language, which has no neuter Gender. But because Bread and Body are of different Genders in the Latin; he that translated it from the Greek should have joined the Article with Panis, if he had not found that the Evangelical Demonstration was made of the Body. Moreover, when Luther confesseth that the same Difference of Gender is in the Greek, he might easily know that when the Evangelists writ in Greek, they would have put in the Article relating to the Bread, if they had not known our Lord's Mind; but they were willing to teach the Christians, by the Article relating to the Body, that, in the Communion, Christ did not give Bread to his Disciples, but his Body.

Wherefore, when Luther, to serve his own Turn, interprets the Words of Christ, take, and eat, this is my Body that is, this Bread he had taken; not I, but Christ himself teacheth us to understand the Contrary, to wit, That what was given them, and seemed to be Bread, was not Bread, but his own Body; if the Evangelists have rightly delivered us the Words of Christ: For otherwise he should say, not Hoc, that it might be expounded for Hie,) but, more properly, Hie Panis est Corpus meum: By which Saying he might teach his Disciples, what Luther now teaches to the whole Church, to wit, That in the Eucharist the Body of Christ, and the Bread are together. But our Savior spoke after that Manner, that he might plainly manifest, that only his Body is in the Sacrament, and no Bread.

How magnificently Luther brings in this for his Argument, That Christ speaks of the Chalice, which no body holds to be transubstantiated P I admire the Man is not ashamed of so unmeasurable a Folly. When Christ says, This Chalice of the New Testament is my Blood, what does that make for Luther? For what else does it signify, but that what he gave his Disciples to drink, was his own Blood? Will Luther make appear, by those Words of Christ, that the Substance of Wine remains, because Christ speaks of Blood? Or that the Wine cannot be changed into Blood, because the Chalice is still there? I wish he had chosen to himself some other Matter in which he might have played and sported with less Danger. For when he so much excuses the Bohemians and Greeks from Heresy; as to call all the Roman Catholics Heretics, he shews himself to be a worse Heretic than either of those; who not only deny the Faith which the whole Church believes, but also persuades People to believe worse than the

Greeks or Bohemians ever did. I have thus far disputed these Things, that I might make appear, that what he brags himself to make out, cannot be shewn by the Words of Christ, and the Evangelists; nay in them the quite contrary is very clear, to wit, that Bread is not in the Eucharist. Luther speaks of the Eucharist s being called Bread, in the Acts of the Apostles: I desire he would shew us the Place: For my Part, I find none that is not ambiguous, and which seems not rather to speak of a common Banquet, then the Sacrament. Yet I confess the Apostle speaks more than once of Bread, following the Custom of Scripture (which sometimes calls a Thing, not by the Name of what it is, but of what it was before; as when it says, the Rod of Aaron devoured the Rods of the Magicians[17]; which then were not rods, but Serpents) or else perhaps content to call it what in Species it appeared to be; deeming it sufficient to feed the People with Manna[18] who as yet were but inexpert in Faith; and at first to exact Nothing of them, but even to believe that the Body of Christ was, after any Manner whatsoever, in the Sacrament; but afterwards, by little and little, to feed them with more solid Meat, as they gathered more Strength in Christ. He might as well have also touched, in the Acts of the Apostles, at that Place where St. Peter, speaking to the people, and insinuating into them the Faith of Christ; yet durst not as yet say any Thing openly of his Divinity: So cautious were they then of exposing rashly the sacred Mysteries to the People. But Christ made no Difficulty to teach his Apostles, (whom he had for so long Time instructed in his own Doctrine,) the very first Time he instituted the blessed Sacrament, that the Substance of Bread and Wine remained no longer in the Sacrament; but that the Forms of both remaining, the Substance was changed into his Body and Blood: Which he so plainly taught, that it is a very strange Thing that any Body should ever after call into Question a Thing so clear in itself.

For how could he have more properly said, that no Bread and Wine remain in the Sacrament, then when he said, this is my Body? for he did not say, my Body is in this, or, with this which you see, is my Body; as if it should consist in the Bread, or with the Bread; but this (says he) is my Body, manifestly declaring, (to shut the Mouth of every yelping Fellow) what he then gave, to be his Body. And though he had called what he gave to the Apostles, by the Name of Bread, (which he did not) yet, when he should teach them that were present, that what he called Bread, was no other Thing but his Body, (into which, by his Will, the Bread was changed) none could doubt what Christ would have us understand by the Name of Bread. And that very Circumstance (for Luther admits Circumstances) evidently declares, that the Word Bread, when the Bread is turned into Flesh, signifies, (without any Violence to the Text,) the Species, not the Substance of Bread; unless Luther will stick so closely to the Propriety of Words, as to believe, that Christ was wheaten, or barley Bread in Heaven; because he says of himself, I am the Bread which descended from Heaven[19]; or that he was a Vine laden with real Grapes, because he said, I am the true Vine, and my Father is the Husbandman[20]; or that the Elect shall be rewarded in Heaven with corporal Pleasures, because Christ said, I dispose unto you a Kingdom, as my Father has disposed unto me; that ye may eat and drink at my Table in my Kingdom..

---

[17] Ex. 7:12
[18] Heb. 5:12
[19] John 6:41
[20] John 15:1, Lu. 22:29-30

Luther takes a deal of Pains to confute the Arguments of the Neoteries, by which they endeavored to maintain and prove Transubstantiation, by philosophical Reasons, out of Aristotle s School; in which he troubles himself more than is requisite: For the Church does not believe it, because they dispute it so to be; but because She believed so from the Beginning, and that none should stagger about it, decreed that all should so believe. They therefore exercise their Wit with philosophical Reasons, that they may be able to teach that no absurd Consequence can follow that Belief; or that the Change of Bread into a new Substance, does not necessarily leave, but take away the former.

Luther says, This Doctrine of Transubstantiation, is risen in the Church within these three Hundred Years; whereas before, for above twelve Hundred Years, from Christ's Birth, the Church had true Faith: Yet all this while was there not any Mention made of this prodigious (as he calls it) Word Transubstantiation. If he strives thus only about the Word, I suppose none will trouble him to believe Transubstantiation; if he will but believe, that the Bread is changed into the Flesh, and the Wine into the Blood; and that Nothing remains of the Bread and Wine but the Species; which, in one Word, is the Meaning of those who put in the Word Transubstantiation. But after the Church decreed that to be true, (though this were the first Time it should be ordained) yet if the Ancients did not believe the Contrary, although none should ever think of that Thing before; why should not Luther be obedient to the present Decree of the whole Church, as persuaded that this is revealed now at length to the Church, which was hidden before? For as the Spirit inspires where he is willing[21]; so likewise, he inspires when he pleases.

But this is no such Thing, as Luther feigns, when he says, this Doctrine of Transubstantiation is risen up within three hundred Years. Yet let it not vex him to allow us four hundred Years; for I think it is so many since Hugo de Sancta Victore wrote a Book of the Sacraments, in which, though not the Word Transubstantiation itself, yet the Sense of his Words you may find to be of the same Effect. Though this Sacrament (says he) is but one, yet three different Things are proposed in it; to wit, the visible Form, the real Presence of the Body, and Virtue of spiritual Grace/ You see how he puts down the Accidents of Bread, not the Substance; and the true Substance of the Body, not the Form ; and more plainly a little further: For what we see is the Species of the Bread and Wine ; but what we believe to be under that Form, is the very Body of Christ which hung on the Cross, and the very Blood which flowed from his Side. He is yet clearer in another Place, where he says, by the Word of Sanctification, the true Substance of Bread and Wine is turned, or changed into the true Body and Blood of Christ, only the Form of Bread and Wine remaining, and the Substance passing into another Substance. By this, then, it appears, that this Doctrine of Transubstantiation is somewhat more ancient than Luther pretends it to be. But, for the better Confirmation of this, we will shew, that what he thinks to be risen within three hundred Years, was the Faith of the holy Fathers above a thousand Years ago: For it is certain, that the Faithful, for above a thou sand Years past, did believe the

---

[21] John 3:8

Substance of Bread and Wine to be truly changed into the Body and Blood of Jesus Christ: Which makes me wonder that Luther is not ashamed of himself, to say, that this Belief of Transubstantiation has not been in the Church above three hundred Years. Who knows not that Eusebius Emissenus dyed above six hundred Years since? who, as if dreading the Broaching of such false Opinions said, let all Doubt or Ambiguity of Unfaithfulness be put away: For he that is the Author of the Gift, is also the Witness of the Truth; now the invisible Priest converteth, by his secret Power, the visible Creatures into his own Body and Blood; saying, take and eat, this is my Body. Does not this holy Man say, most plainly, that the Substance of the Bread and Wine is changed into the Substance of the Body and Blood? What could be said more to the Purpose, then this of St. Augustine? We honor, (says he) invisible Things, viz. the Flesh and Blood in the visible Form of the Bread and Wine: He does not say, in the Bread and Wine, but in the Form of the Bread and Wine. Luther denies that the Form of Bread is to be called Bread; and does he think that St. Austin should call that the Form of Bread, which is the true Substance of Bread? Likewise, St. Gregory Nissenus says, that before the Consecration, it is but Bread; but when it is consecrated by Mystery, it is made, and called the Body of Christ: His saying that it is so, before the Consecration, gives us to understand, that it is not so after the Consecration. Theophilus also, expounding the Words, Hoc est, et cetera. This is my Body, &c. says, This, which now I give, and you receive. For the Bread is not a Figure only of the Body of Christ, but is changed into the proper Body of the Flesh and Blood of Christ; and a while after, if we did see, says he, the Flesh and Blood of Christ, we could not endure to eat them: therefore, our Lord condescending to our Weakness, preserves the Forms of the Bread and Wine; but changeth the Bread and Wine into his own true Flesh and Blood. Luther is here, by this good and learned Man, twice beaten down: For first he teaches, that that Article, Hoc, is not to be understood as Luther interprets it; Hoc, that is, Hic Panis; but Hoc, that is, this which now I give, and ye take: Secondly, he plainly says, that the Form of the Bread and Wine remains, and that the Substance is changed into the Body and Blood. But what else do they mean, who use the Word Transubstantiation, then what Theophilus said, not within three hundred Years, for he was dead some hundred Years before the Word Transubstantiation was used? What need I mention St. Cyril, who not only affirms the same Thing, but almost in the same Words? Tor God, (says he) condescending to our Frail ties, lest we should abhor Flesh and Blood on the holy Altars, infuseth the Force of Life into what is offered, by changing them into the Truth of his own proper Flesh. Moreover, that none should say that the ancient Fathers believed the Body of Christ in such Manner, to be in the Eucharist, as that the Bread should still remain; not only those Things which I have related, do fully evince, (as plainly they do) but likewise what we have above related out of St. Ambrose, when he said, that although the Form of Bread and Wine is seen, nevertheless we are to believe that there is nothing else after the Consecration, but the Body and Blood of Christ.

You see how the Holy Father says, that it is not only the Body and Blood; but that there is nothing be sides them, although the Bread and Wine seem to be there. And he that speaks this, has not said it within three hundred Years past, in which Luther feigns that this Belief of Transubstantiation is risen; but he spoke it above a thousand Years ago: Neither can I believe that any of the ancient Fathers would have approved that fine Comparison of Luther s, viz. of Iron joined with the Fire. For none ever said that Iron is so converted into Fire, that the Form only remains, the Substance of the Iron being changed into that of the Fire; which was the Opinion of all the Ancients concerning Bread and the Flesh of Christ; or if, perhaps, any one Person was of a contrary Sentiment, yet one Swallow makes no Summer: And that Man, whoever he was, is rather to be excused for not perfectly seeing through a Matter, at that Time not in Dispute, then to be imitated, contrary to the Belief of all the rest of the whole Church, and of so many Ages, in a Thing which he, if a good Man, and now alive, without Doubt, would not argue against: For that Man that has so much Esteem for the Body of Christ, as he ought to have, will more easily consent that any other two Substances should remain together, then that any other Body remain, mixed with the adorable Body of Christ; seeing there is no Substance worthy to be mixed with that Substance which created all Substances. Moreover, I suppose that the primitive Fathers would as little approve that Comparison of Luther, by which he intends to prove, that the Bread remains with the Flesh, as God did remain with Man in the Person of Christ: For as the most learned and the most holy of the ancient Fathers confess, in divers Places, that the Bread is changed into Flesh; so none of them were so wicked or ignorant, as to think that the Humanity was changed into the Divinity; unless perhaps Luther will devise a new Person, that as God took on him the Nature of Man, so God and Man take the Nature of Bread, and Wine; which if he believes, he shall be accounted an Heretic, by all those who are not Heretics.

Wherefore, (to conclude this Discourse of Transubstantiation) it evidently appears by Christ s Words, and by the Judgment of the holy Fathers, that the Faith of the Church, at this present, is true, by which it is believed, that the Substance of Bread or Wine doth not remain in the Eucharist; whence it follows, that Luther's Opinion, in teaching the Contrary, is false and heretical: From which Persuasion, I admire what Profit he promises the People: Is it, as Luther says, That no Body should esteem himself an Heretic, if perhaps he should be of his Opinion. But he himself confesses, that there is no Harm in believing this, as the Catholic Church now believes; but on the Contrary, the whole Church takes him to be an Heretic, who is of Luther's Opinion: He, therefore, ought not to move any one whom he wishes well, to be of his Judgment, which is condemned by the whole Church; but rather advise those he loves, to join themselves to those whom he himself witnesses to be in no Danger. That Opinion of Luther is therefore false, as it is against the public Faith, not
only of this Time, but also of all Ages: Nor does he free from Captivity those who believe him; but, drawing them from the Liberty of Faith, that is, from a safe Hold, (as he himself confesses) he captivates them, leading them into a Precipice, into inaccessible, uncertain, doubtful and dangerous Ways: And he that loves Danger, shall perish therein[22].

After this Man, who is free from any Evil, has escaped these two Captivities, which he imagines to himself; that he may not captivate his Mind to the Obedience of God, he overcomes (as he pretends) a third Captivity; and proposes a Liberty by which he may captivate the whole Church. This, worse than sacrilegious calf, endeavors to scatter abroad the Church's most splendid Congregation: to extinguish its Pillar of Fire; to violate the Ark of the Covenant; and to destroy the Chief and only Sacrifice which

---

[22] Eccles. 3:27

reconciles us to God, and which is always offered for the Sins of the People: For, as much as in him lies, he robs the Mass of all the Benefits that flow from it to the People; denying it to be a good Work, or to bring to them any Kind of Profit. In which Thing I know not whether more to admire his Wickedness, or his foolish Hope; or rather his mad Pride; who, seeing so many Obstructions before him, as he himself mentions, brings Nothing with him, whereby to remove the least; but seems as if he would go about to pierce a Rock with a Reed. For he sees, and con fesses himself, that the Opinions of the holy Fathers are against him, as also the Canon of the Mass, with the Custom of the universal Church, confirmed by the Usage of so many Ages, and the Consent of so many People. What Defense then does he oppose against so innumerable, so powerful, and so invincible Armies? His accustomed Force rages; he strives to breed Discord, and move Seditions, to excite the Commonalty against the Nobility: And that he may the more easily stir them up to a Revolt; he, by his foolish and weak Policy, falsely pretends that he has Christ for Captain of the whole Army in the Camp; and that the Trumpet of the Gospel sounds only for him; which is the most ridiculous Stratagem that ever was invented. For what Man living is so wicked or blockish, as to think that the Church, which is the mystical Body of Christ should be in such Manner dilacerated, as that the Head should be severed from the rest of the Members, joined together amongst themselves; or that Christ, who never abandoned the Flesh which once he took, should have cast off the

Church, for whose Sake he took that Flesh; and that he should, for so many Ages, absent himself from her, with whom he promised to remain to the End of the World, and should now pass to Luther's Side, who is her professed Enemy? But pray let us see by what Enchantment he makes it appear for Truth, that Christ is on his Side, as he brags. After many idle Circumstances, he goes about to define what the Mass is; afterward he separates the Ceremonies of the Mass, from the Mass itself; he examines the Lord's Supper, and ponders the Words which Christ used in the Institution of the Sacrament of the Mass: And, having found in them the Word Testament, (as if a Thing very obscure,) he begins to triumph, as though he had conquered his Enemies: He beautifies with Words this his new-found Mystery; (as he calls it) and with great Gravity, as if it was never heard of before, teaches us what a Testament is. He bawls aloud, that it is to be marked and taken notice of, that a Testament is the Promise of a dying Person, by which he bequeaths the Inheritance, and institutes Heirs: Therefore (says he) this Sacrament of the Mass, is no other Thing than the Testament of Christ; and the Testament is Nothing but the Promise of the eternal Heritage giving his Body and Blood to us Christians, whom he appointed for his Heirs, as a Sign for the ratifying his Promise: This he repeats over and over again; he inculcates, and fixes it; intending to make it his immoveable Foundation whereon to build Wood, Hay and Stubble[23]; For, in laying this Ground-work, That Mass is the Testament of Christ, he boasts, that he will destroy all the Wickedness that impious Men (as he says) have conveyed into the Sacrament; and that he will clearly prove we ought to receive the Communion with Faith alone, without much regard to any Manner of Good-works whatsoever; and by how much the more erroneous our Consciences are, and the more moved with the Sting or Titillation of our Sins, the more holy is our State for approaching the Communion: But the more clear, pure and free from the Stain of Sin our Consciences

---

[23] Corn. 3:12

are, in the worse Capacity are we to receive. Further (he says) that Mass is no Sacrifice; that it is only profitable to the Priest, not to the People; that it is nothing available, either to the Dead, or to the Living; that to sing Mass for Sins, for any Necessity, or for the Dead, is an impious Error; that Fraternities, as also the annual Commemorations for the Dead, are vain and wicked Things; that our voluntary maintaining of Priests, Monks, Canons, Brothers, and whatsoever we call religious, is to be abolished. These, therefore, with many other great good Things, he glories to have found out by this Discovery, of the blessed Sacrament being the Testament of Christ. And now he inveighs against the sententious Doctors, as he calls them: He exclaims against all such as preach to the People; Those for writing, these for preaching so much in the Defense of the blessed Sacrament of the Eucharist; and neither of them saying any Thing of the Testament, but most impiously concealing that most incomparable Good from the People, which so long since might have been profitably known. The Laity, (he says) neither alive, nor after Death, will ever receive any Benefit by the Mass: For the Ignorance of which Matter, he denounces all Priests and Monks at this Day in the World, with their Bishops and Superiors, to be Idolaters, and in a very dangerous Condition.

I do not therefore discuss how true that Mystery of Luther is, from which he attributes so much Glory to himself, in applying so accurately his Definition of the Testament to the Sacrament; yet at the same Time, I do not see why he should brag so much of this new Invention of his. I do not know indeed who he hears preach, where he is; but here, I am sure, we have heard Preachers, over and over again, not only treat of those Things, which Luther brings out for so new and exquisite, viz. That Christ is a Testator; that he made his Testament in the last Supper; that he promised an Inheritance, which he declared to be the Kingdom of Heaven; that he instituted the Faithful for his Heirs; that the Sacrament is a holy Sign, exhibited for a Seal; not only these, and such like, but also the dumber of Witnesses, the Bill, and other Rites of Testaments, they unfolded to us out of the deepest Secrets of both Laws, and applied all of them exactly to the Sacrament. And this they did more consciously, and truly, than Luther: For they referred to the same Testament, not only what Christ did at his last Supper, but also what he suffered on the Cross; only in this differing from Luther, that they did not find out the admirable and hitherto unheard-of Benefits of the Mass, by which the Clergy should lose all the Fruits of it in this Life, and the Laity in the Life to come: For the People would not maintain the Clergy to say Mass, if they should be persuaded they could reap no spiritual Good thereby.

But it is worth our While to see from what Tree Luther gathers this Fruit. After he has very often repeated, that the Sacrament of the Eucharist is the Sign of the Testament, and the Testament is nothing else but the Promise of Inheritance; he thinks that it consequently follows, that the Mass cannot be a good Work, or a Sacrifice. To which, if any one consents, he must immediately admit that Catalogue of Plagues, by which he endeavors to confound the whole Face of the Church: But if you deny it, then can he do nothing with so monstrous a Design: For I am almost ashamed of the Arguments, by which he pretends to teach these Things; they are so trifling and frivolous, in a Matter of so great Majesty. Thus, he concludes; (for I will give you his own Words) You have heard that Mass is nothing else but the divine Promise, or Testament of Christ, commended by the Sacrament of his Body and Blood; which, if it be true, you understand, that by any Means it cannot be a Work; nor is it to be used after any other Manner, then by Faith alone; and Faith is not a Work, but the Mistress and Life of Works. It is a strange Thing, that, after so much Pains-taking, he vents nothing but mere Wind: Which, though he would have us believe it to be of Strength to overturn Mountains; yet truly to me, it seems not of Force enough to shake a Reed. For if you withdraw the Coverings of his Words, with which (like an Ape in Purple) he decks this ridiculous Matter; if you take away the Exclamations, whereby he so often rails, and insults, as a Conqueror; (though not as yet entered the Battle against the Church;) or if he had clearly proved the Thing, you will find that nothing remains, but a naked, and miserable Piece of Sophistry. For what else has he said by all that Heap of Words, but that Mass is a Promise, and therefore no Work? Who would but pity this Man, that is so blockish, as not to perceive his own Impertinency; or, if he understands himself, who would but take it heinously from him, that thinks all Christians so dull, as not to discover or comprehend so manifest Follies? I shall not dispute with him about the Testament or Promise, or the whole Definition, or Application thereof to the Sacrament. I will not trouble him so much; he may perhaps find others who will ruin the best Part of his Foundation, by saying, That the Testament is the Promise of the Evangelical Law, as the Old Testament was of the Law of Moses; and by denying it to be rightly handled by Luther/ For neither was the Testator particularly to name what he should leave to the Heir, whom he had appointed over all in general; nor is the Remission of Sins, which Luther says, is bequeathed for an Inheritance, the same with the Kingdom of Heaven, but rather the Way to Heaven. If anyone should urge and press Luther in these, and such-like Sayings, he might, perhaps, by fastening these Engines in any Part of his Structure, shake the whole Frame thereof; but I shall leave that to such as shall be willing to do it: And because he desires his Foundation should remain unshaken, I shall not go about to move it; I will only shew, that the House he has built upon it, falls of itself. And to shew this more plainly, let us consider a little the Original of the Matter, and examine the Mass by its first Pattern.

Christ, in his most holy Supper, in which he instituted this Sacrament, made of Bread and Wine, his own Body and Blood, and gave to his Disciples to be eaten and drunk: A few Hours afterwards, he offered the same Body and Blood on the Altar of the Cross, a Sacrifice to his Father for the Sins of the People; which Sacrifice being finished, the Testament was consummated. Being now near his Death, he did (as some dying Persons are wont to do) declare his Will concerning what he desired should be done afterwards in Commemoration of him. Wherefore, instituting the Sacrament, when he gave his Body and Blood to his Disciples, he said, Do this in Commemoration of me. He who diligently examines this, will find Christ to be the eternal Priest, who, in Place of all the Sacrifices which were offered by the temporary Priesthood of Moses s Law, (whereof many were but the Types and Figures of this holy Sacrifice) has instituted one Sacrifice, the greatest of all, the Plenitude of all, as the Sum of all others, that it might be offered to God, and given for Food to the People: In which Thing, as Christ was the Priest, so his Disciples did for that Time represent the People, who themselves did not consecrate, but received, from the Hands of their Priest, the consecrated Sacrament. But God did shortly after elect and institute them Priests, that they might consecrate the same Sacrament, in Commemoration of him.

And what else then is this, but that they should consecrate, and not only receive it themselves, but likewise give it to the People, and offer it to God? For, if Luther should argue that the Priest cannot offer, because Christ did not offer in his Supper, let him remember his own Words, that a Testament involves in it the Death of the Testator; therefore, has no Force or Power, nor is in its full Perfection; till the Testator be dead. Wherefore, not only those Things which Christ did first at his Supper, do belong to the Testament, but also his Oblation on the Cross: For on the Cross he consummated the Sacrifice which he began in the Supper: And therefore, the Commemoration of the whole Thing, to wit, of the Consecration in the Supper, and the Oblation on the Cross, is celebrated, and represented together in the Sacrament of the Mass; so that it is, the Death that is more truly represented than the Supper. And therefore, the Apostle, when writing to the Corinthians, in these Words, as often as ye shall eat this Bread, and drink this Cup, adds, not the Supper of our Lord, but ye shall declare our Lord's Death[24].

Let us now come to Luther s chief Reasons, by which he proves Mass to be neither good Work, nor Sacrifice. And though it were better first to treat of Sacrifice; yet because he has first moved concerning Work, we will follow him. When therefore he thus argues, Mass is a Promise, therefore no good Work, because no Promise is a Work; we answer, that the Mass, which the Priest celebrates, cannot more properly be called a Promise, than the Consecration of Christ was: And all under one we will demand of him, if Christ did not do a Work, when he consecrated? which if he denies, we shall certainly begin to admire that there should be some Work done by him who cuts an Image out of Wood, and not by Christ, when he made his own Flesh of Bread! And if Christ did any Work, I am certain none will doubt of its being a good Work: For if the Woman, who poured the Ointment upon his Head[25], wrought a good Work in that, who doubts of his performing a good Work, when he gave his Body for our Nourishment, and offered it in Sacrifice to God? If this cannot be denied, unless by him who intends to trifle in so serious a Matter, neither can it also be denied that the Priest worketh a good Work in the Mass; seeing that in the Mass he does nothing else but what Christ did in his last Supper, and on the Cross; for this is declared in Christ's own Words, Do this in Commemoration of me. By which Words, what was he willing they should represent, and do in the Mass, but what he had done himself in his last Supper, and on the Cross? For he instituted, and began the Sacrament at his last Supper, which he perfected on the Cross. And from this Reason especially it seems, was taken the Occasion of mingling Water with the Wine, according to the Custom of the Church; because Water and Blood did flow from the Side of Christ, dying on the Cross.

Since it cannot be denied that Christ wrought a good Work in his last Supper, and on the Cross; neither can it be denied, that the Priest represents, and per forms the same Things in the Mass: How can it then be feigned that the Mass is not a good Work? Wherefore, since Luther so handles the Matter, as to say, That, because the Communion of one Layman does not profit another of the Laity, so neither does the Mass of the Priest profit the People; how dim of Sight is he himself, and how much does he endeavor to spread his Darkness over the Eyes of others, when he sees not that there is this Difference in the Case, That now the Laity receives out of the Priest's

---

[24] 1 Corn. 11:26
[25] Matt. 26:7-10

Hand, as the Apostles did first from Christ's; and the priest performs what Christ did then perform; for he offers to God the same Body that was offered by Christ?

From whence also it appears how cold an Argument is Luther s Comparison of the Mass, with the Sacrament of Baptism or Marriage; endeavoring to prove, that, because one Layman cannot be baptized for another, nor marry a Wife for another Man; so a Priest cannot celebrate Mass for any other Person! For he openly puts Marriage out of the Number of the Sacraments, and Baptism too, under a Color; when he says, that really there is but one Sacrament: Why then does he now compares Baptism and Marriage with the Sacrament of the Mass, if he does not hold them to be Sacraments?

And although he should confess them both to be Sacraments, (as indeed they are) yet is neither of them to be compared to this of the Mass; but in such Manner as this Sacrament, which is the proper Body of him who is Lord of all Sacraments, may have a Prerogative above all other, which he himself made; since it is manifest, that the Priest, in administering all other Sacraments, does Good to all those who receive them; so in this, while he offers it in the Mass, he is profitable, and communicates Good to all.

Otherwise, if Luther exact with such Severity, that all Sacraments should be alike, and no Difference amongst them; and that, in the Sacrament of the Eucharist, the Priest s Condition is no better than that of the Laity; why compels he not the Priest to receive the Communion from the Hands of another, and not suffer him to take it himself, though he can consecrate it; even as he cannot absolve himself, though he has the Keys of Penance?

And what he says of Faith, which he believes all Men are to have in their own Persons, and that not the Priest's, but every Man s own Faith, is that which profits him, even (says he) as Abraham has not believed for all the Jews. I allow it to be very true; yet it proves no more than what it proposes: For neither has Christ himself, offered by himself on the Cross, saved the People, without every Man s particular Faith; that none may think the Mass of any Priest should do it; yet the Mass of every Priest helps those to Salvation, who, by their Faith, have deserved to be Partakers of the greatest Good communicated in the Mass to many.

It may likewise be sometimes advantageous to the procuring the Infusion of Faith into the Unfaithful, as it is procured by the Death and Passion of Christ, that Grace should be given to the Gentiles; by which, through the Hearing of the Word, they might come to the Understanding of the Faith of Christ.

But Luther easily perceives, that it is no hard Matter to destroy what he himself has built, if Mass can be a Sacrifice or Offering, which may be offered to God; he therefore, promises to remove this Obstacle, which, that he may the more easily seem to do, he objects against himself such Things, as he perceives to stand in his Way. And now, (says he) another, the greatest and most spacious of all Scandals, is to be taken away, that is, Mass believed everywhere to be a Sacrifice offered to God; which Opinion the Words of the Canon seem to favor, where it is said these Gifts, these Presents, and these holy Sacrifices; and below that, this Offering. He likewise complains, that it is taken for a Sacrifice, et cetera. From thence Christ is called the Host of the Altar. To this may be added the Words of the holy Fathers, so many Examples, and the constant Custom observed over the whole World.

You see, gentle Reader, what Blocks he himself finds standing in his Way: Take Notice now with what Herculean Strength he undertakes to remove them: But to all these, (says he) are constantly to be opposed the Words and Example of Christ. But pray what Words of Christ are these, which have been unknown to so many holy Fathers in Times past, and to the whole Church of Christ, during so many Ages, and now, by Luther, like a new Esdras, found out? This he declares himself, when he says, for unless we bring it to pass, that Mass be accounted a Promise or Testament, as the Words, clearly make out; we lose the whole Gospel, and all Comfort: These are his Words: It now remains that we see his Example. f Christ, says he, at his last Supper, when he instituted this Sacrament, and bequeathed the Testament, offered it not to God the Father, and has not performed it as a good Work for others; but sitting at the Table, he proposed the same Testament, and exhibited a Sign to every one of them. Those are therefore the Words of Christ! This is the Example, by which, now at last, only Luther himself clearly sees Mass neither to be a Sacrifice, nor Offering! It is a Wonder that, of so many holy Fathers, of so many Eyes which have read the Gospel in the Church for so many Ages, none was ever so quick-sighted, as to perceive a Thing so apparent; and that at this present Time they are all so blind, as not to discern what Luther (though he points it out with his Finger,) brags so clearly to see himself! Is not Luther rather mistaken, and thinks himself to see something, which in Reality he sees not, or endeavors to shew us with his Finger, that which is no-where to be found? For pray what Sort of Proof is that where he undertakes to teach that Mass is no Sacrifice, because it is a Promise. as if Promise and Sacrifice were as repugnant together as Heat and Cold? Which Reason of his is altogether so weak, that it seems not worthy an Answer. For the so many Sacrifices of Moses s Laws, though all Figures of Things to come, yet were they Promises in themselves, promising the Things for which they were done; not only the Future, of which they were Figures, but also Deliverances, Expiations, Purgations and Purifications, of the People then present, for whom they were solemnly offered every Year. Which Thing being so apparent, that it leaves no Plea for Ignorance, makes Luther s Dissimulation appear altogether ridiculous; when arguing that this Thing cannot be done; which not only he himself, but all the People know to have been so often performed.

So come we to the Example of Christ, by which Luther thinks he so vehemently oppresses us; because Christ, in his last Supper, did not use the Sacrament for a Sacrifice, nor has he offered it to his Father: Out of which he goes about to prove, That the Mass, which ought to agree with the Example of Christ, by whom it was instituted, cannot be a Sacrifice or Offering.

If Luther so rigidly summons us to the Example of our Lord's Supper, as not to permit the Priest to do any Thing that we do not read Christ to have done in it; then must they never receive themselves in the Sacrament which they consecrate: For we do not read in the Gospel, where it mentions the last Supper of our Lord, that our Lord himself received his own Body: and though some Doctors, and the whole Church, do hold that he did receive it: yet that makes nothing for Luther, who discredits not only all the Doctors, but the Faith of the whole Church; and thinks not any Thing to be believed, but what is confirmed by Scriptures, and that clearly to; (for so he writes in the Sacrament of Orders.) In which Sort of Scripture, I am of Opinion, he will not find that Christ received his own Body at his last Supper. Whence it will follow, as I have said, that the Priests ought not to take what they consecrate themselves, if he binds us so strictly to the Example of the last Supper. But if then he allows that the Priests are to receive, because the Apostles did so; and that he holds they are commanded to do what the Apostles did then, not what Christ has done; then must they never consecrate; for Christ , and not the Apostles, did then consecrate. The Matter itself shews, that, in this, the Priests do not only perform what Christ did in his last Supper, but also what he has afterwards done on the Cross; the Apostles leaving us some Things by Tradition, which Christ either never did, or which we do not read that he had done; as the Ceremonies and Signs used in the Consecration, of which I believe most are delivered down to us from the Apostles themselves. Furthermore, they repeat some Words in the Canon of the Mass, as if spoken by Christ himself, which are not read in Scripture; and yet there is no Doubt but he spoke them; for many Things were said and done by Christ, which are not recorded by any of the Evangelists, but by the fresh Memory of those who were present: delivered afterwards, as it were, from Hand to Hand, from the very Times of the Apostles, down to us. Luther doubts not, that Christ said in his last Supper, as often as ye shall do this, ye shall do it in Commemoration of me: And he is so sure that they were Christ s Words, that, from thence he takes his Argument; That Nobody is obliged to receive the Sacrament; but that it is left to every Man's Discretion, and that we are only bound, as often as we do it, to do it in Remembrance of Christ. These very Words he does not read in the Evangelists concerning the Supper of our Lord: For no other Thing is read there, but, do this in Commemoration of me.

Where then read he these, as often as ye shall do these Things? Whether, not in the Mass? Indeed, I believe nowhere else. For the Apostles Words are not so: Wherefore, seeing he trusts so much in these Words, and uses them, because he finds them in the Canon; why does he not give so much Credit to that Part of the same Canon, in which Mass is called an Offering, and Sacrifice?

Wherefore, if he confess that the Priests do rightly receive what they consecrate in the Mass, though no clear Scripture (which only he admits of,) testifies Christ to have done it at his last Supper, nor in any other Place ; he ought not to wonder if the Priest offers Christ to his Father ; which Christ himself has done on the Cross, as it is witnessed by clear Scripture in several Places: For Luther s, own Arguments demonstrate, that the Cross belongs to the Testament made at the Supper, when he says, That the Testament involves the Death of the Testator, by which alone it can be made perfect. Moreover, it seems, as is said, that the mingling of Water with the Wine, had its Beginning from no other Place; which Thing is not said by Scripture to be done at the last Supper, but on the Cross. Let Luther, therefore, forbear to oppose his trifling Argument, That, because Christ at his last Supper did not offer himself, therefore the Priest must not be believed to offer him in the Mass: In which he not only represents what Christ performed in his last Supper, but also, what he did on the Cross, on which he consummated what he began in the Supper.

But now come we to the last of Luther s Arguments; by which, as by a sacred Anchor, his Ship is sustained: Arid this is the most frivolous of all the rest. How can it be, (says he) that the Priest should offer to God what he takes himself? It is not likely (says he) Mass should be a Sacrifice, when we receive it ourselves. The same Thing cannot be received and offered at one and the same Time, nor given and received by one and the same Person. Luther deters us every-where from philosophical Reasonings, when he, in so sacred a Thing, endeavors to sustain himself by the merest Sophistry in the World. For pray was there ever a Sacrifice in Moses s Law, which was not taken by those who offered it? Or did God himself eat what they offered him? Shall I eat the Flesh of Bulls., or drink the Blood of Goats, saith the Lord[26]? Besides, if Christ was both Priest and Sacrifice; why could he not institute that the Priest, who should supply the same Sacrifice, might both offer and receive the Victim himself? But lest I may seem, in this Case, to imitate Luther, who has nothing to say for himself, but what issues out of his own idle Brain; I will lay before you what St. Ambrose says to the Mass, O Lord God, (says he) with how great Contrition of Heart, with what Fountains of Tears, with how great Reverence and Fear, with what Chastity and Purity of Mind that divine and celestial Mystery is to be celebrated : Where thy Flesh is truly received; where thy Blood is truly drank; where the lowest is joined to the highest; and divine Things with human: Where the Saints and Angels are present; where, after an admirable and unspeakable Manner, thyself are both Priest and Sacrifice! Who shall be able to celebrate this Mystery worthily, if then Almighty God do not render him worthy that offers? You see how the holy Father, in this Place, calls Mass an Oblation, and says that Christ himself is both Priest and Sacrifice in it, even as he was on the Cross. Let Luther see how much he attributes to this Man's Authority; but St. Gregory makes appear how much he had him in Esteem, when, in this Manner, he imitated him in his Writings: Which of the Faithful (says he) can doubt, but that in the very Time of the Immolation, the Heavens are opened to the Words of the Priest, in that Mystery of Christ: That Choirs of Angels are present; that the lowest Things are associated to the highest: That Earth is joined with Heaven; and that of Visible and Invisible is made one Thing? And in another Place, for this singular Victim, which renews to us the Death of the only Be gotten, does loose our Souls from eternal Death. Nor speaks he less to the Purpose, when he says, hence therefore let us ponder with ourselves, how much that Sacrifice stands us instead, which always imitates the Passion of the only begotten Son/ We see, that not only St. Ambrose, but also St. Gregory, calls Mass an Immolation and Sacrifice; and confesses, that, not only the last Supper of Christ, (as Luther holds) but also his Passion is represented in it.

But these Fathers alone were not of that Judgment, for St. Augustine confesses the same Thing, in divers Places, who says thus of the Mass, The Oblation is every Day renewed, though Christ has but once suffered: Because we daily fall, therefore is Christ daily offered for us. Also, the Eucharist is a blessed Offering by which we are blessed; an Enrollment, by which we all are enrolled in Heaven; a Ratification, whereby we are mustered in the Bowels of Christ.

Seeing, therefore, that Mass is by so holy and learned Men called an Offering, and a Sacrifice; and that they are of Opinion, that not only the last Supper of Christ, but also,

---

[26] Ps. 49:13

his Passion is by it commemorated; that they confess so immense and great Advantages to proceed from it; and that the Church, agreeing with them, sings the same in the whole Mass: I much admire with what Face Luther dares to cry out, on the Contrary, that Mass is no Sacrifice or Offering; and that it brings no Profit to the People; deriding the Authority of so many holy Fathers, or rather of the whole Church, by his most vain Device; as if they were all Things, which were understood of the Relics of the Jewish Cere monies, (in which he says, the Priest did heave up what was offered by the People) Which Comment of Luther s did seem so foolish and absurd, even to himself, that he doubted whether he should withstand the Sentiments of the holy Fathers, and the Customs of the whole Church, by such a babbling Argument, or rather openly despise them: For, says he, what shall we say to the Canons and Authorities of the Fathers? I answer, says he, that if we have nothing at all to say against them; it is safer to deny all Things, than to confess that Mass is a Work or Sacrifice, lest we deny the Words of Christ, corrupting them together with the Mass. Nevertheless, that we may agree with them also, we will say that all these Things were the Relics of Jewish Ceremonies. Lest, therefore, there should be nothing said, this civil Man, tendering the Repute of the holy Fathers, and the Honor of the whole Church, (lest they might be thought to speak foolishly) will seem to oblige them, by covering their Shame with the Veil of his most excellent Devices, concerning the Relics of the Jewish Rites; which, if any Body remove, it will be to their Danger. For Luther does not ingeniously apprehend, that if any one urges him more narrowly, he would rather blow away all the Testimonies of the holy Fathers, and the Customs of the Church, then that he should allow Mass to be a good Work, or a Sacrifice; that is, rather than allow that to be true which is true: Tor in that (he says) they deny Christ s Words, and corrupt Faith with Mass, who affirm Mass to be a Sacrifice: I suppose that none will believe him, unless he first shews that he has read another Gospel different from that the holy Fathers ever read, or that in reading the same, he has been more diligent than they, or has better understood it; or finally, that he is more careful about Faith, then ever any Man before him was.

But I believe he will not prefer any other Gospel unto us; nor, if he does, will it be admitted, though an Angel from Heaven should descend with it. And that which he proffers, has not been more diligently examined, nor more narrowly proved into by him, than it has been tried and searched into by others heretofore; of whom none ever said, that they found in it what he boasts himself to have found, viz. That Mass is not a good Work; that it is not an Oblation, nor a Sacrifice. Lastly, if any one diligently considers what has been written by the one and the other, he cannot be ignorant what Difference has been in their Care about Faith: Those holy ancient Fathers have observed, that, as this is the chiefest of all Sacraments, as containing in it the Lord of Sacraments; so is it the only Sacrifice, which alone remains, instead of so many Sacrifices of the Old Law; and lastly, of all the Works that can be done for the Salvation of the People, this, without Comparison,

is the best and most wholesome. For when other Sacraments are only profitable to particular Persons receiving them: This, in the Mass, is beneficial to all, in general. And when Prayers made to God by one Man for another, may not only be hindered, but also rendered ineffectual, through the Fault of Men; the merciful Bounty of God has instituted Mass for the Salvation of the Faithful; in which his own Body should be offered a Sacrifice so wholesome, that the Wickedness of the Minister, be it never so great, is not able to lessen, or avert the Benefit of it from the People.

The most holy Fathers seeing these Things, took all possible Care, and used their utmost Endeavors, that the greatest Faith imaginable should be had towards this most propitiatory Sacrament; and that it should be worshipped with the greatest Honor possible: And for that Cause, amongst many other Things, they, with great Care, delivered us this also; That the Bread and Wine do not remain in the Eucharist, but is truly changed into the Body and Blood of Christ. They taught Mass to be a Sacrifice, in which Christ himself is truly offered for the Sins of Christian People: And so far, as it was lawful for Mortals, they adorned this immortal Mystery with venerable Worship, and mystical Rites: They commanded the People to be present in Adoration of it, whilst it is celebrated, for the pro curing of their Salvation. Finally, lest the Laity, by forbearing to receive the Sacrament, should, by little and little, omit it f or-good-and-all; they have established an Obligation that every Man shall receive at least once in a Year. By those Things, and many of the like Nature, the holy Fathers of the Church, in several Ages, have demonstrated their Care for the Faith amid Veneration of this adorable Sacrament. Luther ought not therefore to boast (what nevertheless he does) that they who call Mass a Sacrifice, or say that it is profit able to any, but to him who receives the Sacrament in it, does corrupt the Word of Christ, Faith, and Mass itself.

But it will not be amiss, to consider after what Manner Luther sustains upon his Shoulders the Word of Christ, Faith, and Mass itself, that they may not be come corrupted, or fall. First of all, he changes the Name itself of the Sacrament, into a worse; and that which was, for so many Ages, called the Eucharist, or the Sacrament of Christ s Body, lest the Name of it should put the Auditors in Mind of the Majesty of it, he commands to be called Bread: Afterwards the Bread and Wine, which the Ancients held to be turned into the Body and Blood of our Lord, are by Luther taught to remain entire; that so, by little and little, he may traduce the Honor from Christ to the Bread. After this, though he does not condemn the Church for having adorned and amplified Mass, with Rites and Ceremonies; yet he thinks it should be more Christian-like, if the Pomp of Vestments, Singing, Gestures and other Ceremonies were laid aside; that so it might be more like and near to the first Mass of all, which Christ celebrated in his last Supper with his Apostles; or rather, that nothing may be left that might move the simple Minds of the vulgar Sort, and bring them to the Worship of this invisible Deity, through the Majesty of visible Honor. Moreover, he teacheth, and as much as in him lies, inculcates, that Mass is not a good Work, not a Sacrifice, not an Oblation, nor profitable to any of the People. To what Purpose pray is this so evangelical a Lecture? It is, that all the People, leaving Mass to the Priest, (to whom alone they must be persuaded that it is profitable) may themselves neglect it, and pay no Duty to a Thing unprofitable to them. Lastly, that when they communicate, if they only have but Faith, that they are about to receive the Testament; whatsoever Consciences they bring; nay, the more erroneous they are, and the more troubled with the Sting and Concupiscence of Sin, the more are they to assure themselves that they are Partakers of the divine Promises; especially, because this Sacrament is the Medicine of Sins past, present, and to come; which would find no Room for itself in those who should purge themselves with greatest Anxiety from the Diseases of Sin; and, according to the Precept of the

Apostle, proving themselves[27],* they may approach our Lord's Table with as pure and sincere a Conscience as may be possible; that seeing they cannot say we are justified, at least they may say we are guilty of nothing to ourselves. After Luther, therefore, has taught this short and compendious Preparation for receiving the Eucharist, to wit, in the Faith alone of the Promise; without any good Works, and a light Examination of Conscience; he, that nothing be wanting to the absolute Sanctity of receiving the Sacrament; shews his Desire concerning what Time, and how often he is willing the People should be obliged to receive; and that is, in no Time at all. And why so? What? Is there any one so blind, as not to see what this so palpable a Matter drives at? Certainly nothing else, but that the People may, by Degrees, quite give over communicating at all; who at first changed the daily receiving, into a Seventh-day communicating; and after, to a longer Time; and at last would forsake it altogether; if the Fathers, fearing that should happen, had not decreed, that every Man should receive thrice in a Year; threatening, that he who would not obey, should not be accounted a Christian: Yet nevertheless that Custom could they not continue long; so that, at last, the Matter fell so low, that it could descend no lower; for now, we are obliged to receive but once in a Year: Which Custom, if Luther could demolish, as he endeavors, the World would long (through the Decay of the Fervor of Faith) be reduced to what it should have come to long ago, if it had not been pre vented by this solemn Custom of receiving every Year; that at last there would scarce remain the least Foot step of the Communion amongst the People, nor perhaps, among the Clergy neither, if Luther could bring it about that Mass should be so spoiled, not only of its Preparation and Ceremonies, but also of the People's Resort, Hope and Veneration to it. These are the excellent Promises of Luther; this is that spacious Liberty he promises to all those who forsake the Catholic Church to follow him, viz. That they may be freed at last from the Use and Faith of the Sacrament! Where fore, I forbear to speak any more of this Thing, as being so clear in itself, that it needs no further Dispute. And seeing we have discovered the crafty Winding of the subtle Serpent; which being now seen, (as without Doubt they are by all who are not quite blind) it is not necessary to exhort any Body to shun such apparent Evils. I believe none are so mad, as to forsake the Church of God, for the Synagogue of Satan. That, shunning the Service of Christ, (to serve whom is to reign) he may list himself into the Liberty proposed by Luther; where, under the Name of Liberty, he should willfully, and to his own Knowledge put his Foot into the Snare of the Devil. But rather let all the Faithful of Christ say with the Psalmist, we will not decline from thy Judgments, because thou hast appointed us a Law.[28]

---

[27] 1 Con. 9:28
[28] Ps. 118, 102

CHAPTER V
On Baptism

As for the rest of the Sacraments, it is not necessary to stand long upon them; most of them he takes quite away from us: And the Sacrament of the Eucharist, (being almost the only one he vouchsafed to leave us) has by him been handled in such a Manner, as we have already shown you; so that none can doubt but he de vised by little and little, to demolish this also: or does he praise any one of the Sacraments, unless to the Prejudice of another; for he so much extols Baptism, that he depresses Penance: Though he has treated of Baptism itself after such a Manner, that it had been better he had not touched it at all. For first of all, that he might seem to treat with a great deal of Sanctity in a Matter so holy, he, by a long Discourse, teaches that the divine Promise is to be believed, by which he promises Salvation to them who believe, and are baptized. He is angry, and reproaches the Church for not teaching this Faith to the Christians; as if in any Place they were so ignorant of Christian Faith, as not to understand this: And yet Luther proposes it for a new Thing, almost never before heard of, to the Reproach of all the Doctors.

But this is no new Method of his Proceedings, to trifle in Things known, as though they had before never been heard of. And having in many Words shewn what this Faith is, he afterwards extols the Riches of Faith, to the End he may render us poor of good Works, without which (as St. James saith[29]) Faith is altogether dead.

But Luther so much commends Faith to us, as not only to permit us to abstain from good Works; but also encourages us to commit any Kind of Action, how bad so-ever: Tor (says he) you see now how rich the baptized Man is, who cannot lose his Salvation, though willing to do it, by any Sin whatsoever, except Infidelity: For no Sins can damn him, but only Incredulity. O most impious Doctrine, and Mistress of all Impiety! so

---

[29] James 2:17-26

hateful in itself to pious Ears, that there is no need to confute it: Adultery will not damn then! Murder will not damn! Perjury will not damn! Is not Parricide damnable neither, if everyone believe that he shall be saved, through the Virtue of the Promise alone in Baptism? For this he openly asserts; nor do the Words, which he presently adds, correct this Sentence in any wise; but rather add to the Force of it: For he saith, That all other Things, if Faith return, or stand in the divine Promise made by the Baptized, are swallowed in a Moment in the same Faith; rather by the Truth of God, for he cannot deny himself, if you confess him, and stick faithfully to his Promise: By which Words, what else does he say, but what he has said before, that, Infidelity excepted, all other Crimes are in a Moment swallowed up by Faith alone; if you confess Christ, and stick faithfully to his Promise; that is, if you firmly believe that you are to be saved by Faith, what so-ever you do notwithstanding. And that you may the less doubt what he aims at, Contrition (says he) and Confession of Sins, as also Satisfaction, and all these human Inventions, will forsake you, and leave you the unhappier, if you busy yourselves with them, for getting this divine Truth. What Truth Pray? This that no Sins can damn thee, but Infidelity only/ What Christian Ears can with Patience hear the pestilentious Hissing of this Serpent, by which he extols Baptism, for no other End, but to depress Penance, and establish the Grace of Baptism for a free Liberty of Sinning? Contrary to which, is that Sentence of St. Jerome, which says, that Penance is the Table after Ship-wreck: But this agrees not with Luther; for he denies Sin to be the Ship-wreck of Faith, and disputes it, as if that only Word should totally destroy all the Strength of Faith. But beside Luther, who is ignorant that a Sinner not only Is not saved by the only Faith of Baptism, but also that the Baptism will add to his Damnation? And indeed deservedly; because he has offended God, from whom he had the whole Grace of Baptism, and God exacts the more from him to whom he has given the more: Therefore, since Faith becomes dead by wicked Works, why can it not be said, that he suffers Ship-wreck who falls from the Grace of God, into the Hands of the Devil? From which, without Penance, he cannot escape, or be renewed to such a Condition that Baptism may be profitable to him. Has St. Jerome written wickedly in this? Does the whole Church follow an impious Opinion, for not believing Luther, that Christians are safe enough by Faith alone, in the midst of their Sins, without Penance? Moreover, he is so taken up with the Faith of the Sacrament, that he cares not much for the Form of Words; though, nevertheless, the Word, by which the Water is signified, ought to be of no less Moment, than the Water itself; in which, if he thinks that any Care is to be taken, that it may be pure and elementary; ought not some true Form also be carefully instituted, and used, as is approved, and now observed in the Church, and was formerly in Use amongst the Ancients?

After this, he so magnifies Faith, that he seems almost to intimate, that Faith alone is sufficient without the Sacrament. For in the mean While, he deprives the Sacrament of Grace; he says, that the Sacrament it self-profits nothing; denies that the Sacraments confer any Grace; or that they are effectual Signs of Grace; or that the Sacraments of the Evangelical Law differ in any Kind from those of the Mosaical Law, as touching the Efficacy of Grace: Which Matter I shall not much dispute: But yet, it seems to me, that as all Things were but Figures with the Jews, (the Truth of which we have in the Christian Law) it may not be absurd to believe, that the Sacraments which the Church uses, do so far excel those of the Synagogues, as the new Law surpasses the old; that is, as much as the Body is more excellent than the

Shadow: Nor am I the first, or only Man of this Opinion. For Hugo de Sancto Victore, whom none esteems other than a good and learned Man, has spoken thus; We say, that all Sacraments are certain Signs, and spiritual Graces which by them are conferred. Moreover, that the Signs of spiritual Graces, according to the Process of Time, ought to be framed more evident and plain, that the Knowledge of Truth might increase with the Effect of Salvation. And a little further, Because Circumcision could only lop off exterior Enormities, but not cleanse the inward Eilth of Pollutions, a washing Font of Water succeeded Circumcision, which purgeth the whole, that perfect Justice may be signified. I hope nobody will deny, that this Doctor is of Opinion, That the Sacrament of Baptism cleanses internally, and more efficaciously signifies perfect Justice, then ever Circumcision did. In which Matter Luther takes Notice of two Opinions, and refutes both: The first is, of many who have supposed some secret and hidden Virtue to be in the Word and Water, which should work the Grace of God in the Soul of the Baptized: The other is, of those who attribute no Virtue to the Sacraments, but were of Opinion, That Grace was conferred by God alone, who, according to his Covenant, is present to the Sacraments instituted by himself. But because all agree in this, That Sacraments are efficacious Signs of Grace, Luther rejects the one as well as the other: For my Part, as I do not know which of the Opinions is the truest, so neither dare I be so bold as to contemn either of them. For that very Opinion which now is the less assented to, to wit, That the Water, by Virtue of the Word, has an occult Power of purging the Soul; seems not to be altogether absurd. For if we believe, that Fire has any Influence over the Soul, either to punish or purge Sins; what hinders, that Water should, by the Power of God, (by whom also the other Thing is done) penetrate to wash away the Uncleanness of the Soul? Which Opinion seems to be much confirmed by the Words of St. Augustine, when he says, The Water of Baptism toucheth the Body, and washes the Heart? and also that of St. Beda, who says, That Christ, by the Touch of his most pure Flesh, has given the Water a regenerate Power. Likewise, that of the Prophet Ezekiel seems to incline towards this, I washed thee with Water, and cleansed thy Blood from thee[30]: Which Words, though they were spoken in Times past, before Baptism was instituted, are, notwithstanding, (according to the Custom of the Prophets) understood of the future. Neither speaks he only of the washing of the Body, in which nothing is worthy the Predication of a Prophet; nor was ever any other Washing which washed the Crimes of the Soul, but the Sacrament of Baptism, of which Ezekiel seems to have spoken in the Person of God; prophesying, that there should be a future Cleansing in the Sacrament of Baptism, by the washing Font of Water: Which, by the same Prophet is more plain a little after, when he speaks of the future; I will pour out, saith he, clear Water upon you, and I will cleanse you from all your Iniquities[31]. Whether does he not here promise a Cleansing by Water? Yet Zecharias seems to unfold the Matter more apparently, when he says, Living Water shall flow out from Jerusalem, the one Half to the Eastern Sea, and the other Half to the great Sea[32]. Does not this Discourse manifest unto us the Figure of Baptism, viz. Water flowing from the Church, which should purge both original and actual Sin? which he does not call dead, but living; that he might demonstrate, as I suppose,

---

[30] Ez. 16:9
[31] Ez. 36:25
[32] Rom. 11:33

That, by the secret Sanctification of God, the Force of spiritual Life is infused into a corporeal Element. Although I do not presume to judge, (as I have said already,) nor am I curious, after what Manner God infuses Grace by the Sacraments, because his Ways are inscrutable[33]. Yet I believe, that by one Way or other, this Water should not be idle, where he fore-tells so many, and so great Things, were to be done by Water; especially, since Water, Salt, and other corporeal Things, do receive spiritual Force, by the Word of God, without the Sacrament of Faith; unless all those Things should be spoken in vain; in which Lights, Fire, Water, Salt, Bread, the Altar, Vestments, and Kings, are either adjured by Exorcisms, or blessed by the Invocation of Grace.

If those Things, I say, receive any Virtue or Presence of the Divinity, without the Sacrament; how much more credible is it, that the Water flowing from Christ's Side, does infuse a spiritual Power of Life into the Fountain of Regeneration? Of which Christ himself says, that he, who is not born again of Water, and of the Holy Ghost, shall not enter into the Kingdom of Heaven; to which (as the Apostle saith) we are called in Baptism[34] In which Baptism, I am not against Luther, for having attributed so much to Faith: But, on the other Side, I would not have him attribute so much thereto, as by it to defend an evil Life, or exterminate the Sacraments, which it ought to form. But when he requires that certain and indubitable Faith in the Receiver of the Sacraments; for my Part, I think it is rather to be wished for, than exacted. For I do not doubt, but when St. Peter did exhort the People after this Manner, Do Penance, and be baptized every one of you, in the Name of Jesus Christ; and receive you the Gift of the Holy Ghost unto the Remission of Sins[35] I doubt not but he was ready to receive all the People to Baptism; yet not so suddenly to have exacted that high, certain and indubitable Faith of Luther from them, which none would have been able to have known himself to have attained to: But he promised Remission of Sins, and Grace from the Sacrament itself, to all those who should but only present themselves, and desire it: For an undoubted and certain Faith, is a very great Thing, which happens not always, nor to everybody; no, not perhaps to them who do not doubt but they have it. I indeed shall not doubt to hope, but the Benignity of God assists in his Sacraments, and by Means of visible Signs, infuses invisible Grace; and helps the Tepidity of Believers, by the Fervor of his Sacraments: That many obtain Salvation by the Sacraments, who can promise no more to themselves of their Faith, than he could, who said, Lord I believe, help my Unbelief[36]. In which Thing if any, beside my Adversary, think I attribute too much to the Sacrament; let him know, I define Nothing, I appoint Nothing, in any Case, which may be prejudicial to Faith, from which I derogate Nothing: But as I do not think, that Faith alone, without the Sacrament, is sufficient for him who may receive it; so, neither can the Sacrament suffice him without Faith; but that both ought to concur and co-operate with their Power: And I think it safer to allow Something to the Sacrament, than, like Luther, to attribute so much to Faith, as to leave neither Grace, nor the Efficacy of a Sign to the Sacrament.

Besides, he makes Faith nothing else but a Cloak for a wicked Life, as we have before

---

[33] Zach. 14:8, Jn. 3:5
[34] 1 Corn. 1
[35] Acts 2:38
[36] Mk. 9:23

more fully declared: And that this may the more appear, after he has deprived the Sacraments of Grace, he robs the Church of all Vows and Laws; nor does it at all move him, that God said, Vow, and render to God your Vows[37]. But as for Vows, I make no Doubt but some of those, whom he calls Vovists and Votaries, will undertake to make Answer for their own Profession: For at once, he turns them almost all together, out of the Church.

But, as for the Laws, I admire, that he could, for Shame, invent such ridiculous Things; as if Christians could not sin; but that so great a Multitude of Believers should be so perfect, that nothing needed to be ordered, either for the Honor of God, or the avoiding of Wicked ness. But by the same Work and Policy he robs Princes and Prelates, of all Power and Authority; for what shall a King or a Prelate do, if he cannot appoint any Law-, or execute the Law which was before appointed; but, even like a Ship without a Rudder, suffer his People to float without Land? Where then is that Saying of the Apostle, let every Creature be subject to the higher Powers[38]? Where is that other of his, if thou dost Evil, fear the King, it is not without Reason that he carries the Sword? f Where is also that, be obedient to your Governors, whether to the King as excel ling[39]? And what follows? Why then does St. Paul say, The Law is good[40]? and in another Place, The Law is the Bond of Perfection?

Furthermore, why does St. Augustin say, The Power of the King, the Right of the Owner, the Instruments of the Executioner, the Arms of the Soldier, the Discipline of the Governor, and the Severity of a good Father, were not instituted in vain? The first have all their Customs, Causes, Reasons, Profits; and when the cothers are feared, evil Men are restrained from doing Evil, and the Good live quietly amongst the Wicked:

But I forbear to speak of Kings, lest I should seem to plead my own Case. I only ask this, that if none, either Man or Angel, can appoint any Law among Christians, why does the Apostle institute for us so many Laws; as for electing Bishops; for Widows;) covering the Heads of Women, et cetera? Why has he ordained that a Christian Woman should not forsake her Husband, though an Infidel, if she be not by him first abandoned?[41] Why dares he say, I myself speak to the rest, not the Lord[42]? Why has he exercised so great Power, as to command the Incestuous to be delivered over to Satan, to the Destruction of the Flesh[43]? Why has St. Peter strucken Ananias and Saphira his Wife with the like Punishment, for reserving to themselves a little of their own Moneys? If the Apostles did, of themselves, beside the especial Command of our Lord, appoint so many Things to be observed by Christians, why may not those who succeed them, do the same for the Good of the People? St. Ambrose, Bishop of
Millan, a holy Man, (not arrogant) has scrupled, in commanding that married Persons, through his whole Diocese, should abstain from their lawful Pleasures, during the

---

[37] Ps. 75:12, Eccl. 5:3
[38] Hom. 13:1, Rom. 13:4
[39] Heb. 13:17, 1 Corn. 11:5
[40] 1 Tim 1:8; Prov. 13:14, 1 Cor. 7:12-13
[41] Col. 3:14, 1 Coen. 7:12
[42] 1 Tim. 3, Tit. 1:7, Corn. 5:4-5
[43] 1 Tim. 5:3

whole Time of Lent. And does Luther take it so heinously that the Pope of Rome, Successor of St. Peter, Christ's Vicar, (to whom, as to the Prince of the Apostles, it is believed that Christ gave the Keys of the Church, that by him the rest should enter, or be kept out) should institute a Fast or Prayers? As for his persuading Men to obey outwardly in Body, but yet to retain to themselves their Liberty in Mind, who is so blind as not to see his Shifts and Quirks? Why carries this simple Man, this Hypocrite, both Water and Fire? Why does he (as it were in the Words of the Apostle) command not to serve Men, not to be subject to the Statutes of Men[44]; 1 and yet, notwithstanding, command to shew Obedience to the unjust Tyranny of the Pope? Does the Apostle preach after this Manner? Kings have no Right over you, yet suffer you an unjust Empire. Masters have no Right of Power over you, yet suffer an unjust Servitude. If Luther is of Opinion, that People ought not to obey; why does he say they must obey? If he thinks they ought to obey, why is not he himself obedient? Why does this Quack juggle thus? Why does he thus reproachfully raise himself against the Bishop of Rome, whom he says we ought to obey? Why raises he this Tumult? Why excites he the People against him, whose Tyranny, (as he calls it) he says is to be endured? Indeed, I believe, it is for no other End, then to procure to himself the good Esteem of such Malefactors as desire to escape the Punishment due to their Crimes; that so they might choose him for their Head, who now fights for their Liberty; and demolish Christ's Church, so long founded upon a firm Rock; erecting to themselves a new Church, compacted of flagitious and impious Persons, contrary to that Exclamation of the Prophet, I will have abhorred the Church of Evil-doers, and I not sit with the Impious[45]: Direct me in thy Truth; for thou art God my Savior, and thee have I sustained all Day long.

---

[44] 1 Cor. 7:23
[45] Ps. 25:5, Ez. 18:27

CHAPTER VI
Of the Sacrament of penance

It troubles me exceedingly to hear how absurd, how impious, and how contradictory to themselves the Trifles and Babbles are, wherewith Luther bespatters the Sacrament of Penance. First, after his old Custom, he proposes for a new Thing, what is by everybody commonly known, viz. That we ought to believe the Promise of God, whereby he promiseth to those who repent, Remission of Sins: And then he cries out reproachfully against the Church, for not teaching this Faith. Who I pray you, exhorts any one to the Penance of Judas; that is, to be sorry for what he has committed, and not expect Pardon? Who should tell us, that we ought to pray for Remission of Sins, if he did not teach Pardon to be promised to the Penitent? What is more frequently preached than the Clemency of Almighty God, which is so great, that he mercifully extends it to all Persons who are willing to reform their wicked Lives? Did nobody, beside Luther, ever read, that at what Time soever a Sinner repents of his Sins, he shall be saved[46]? Has none ever read, that the Adulteress was dismissed? That the Prophet was pardoned, who was not only guilty of Adultery, but of Murther also?[47] That

---

[46] Ps. 25:5, Jn. 8:3
[47] 2 Ki. 12, Lu. 23:43

Paradise was given to the Thief on the Cross; and at that Time too, when he could not cancel his Crimes committed, by any Satisfaction? They who in struct the People, are so far from not teaching them this Hope of obtaining Pardon, which Luther cries is past, that they rather seem to do it too much; the People being so easily inclined to rely upon this Confidence, that there is a greater Need of recalling them to the other Side; whereby they may contemplate the severe and inflexible Justice of God: For there are ten to be found, who sin in the too much Confidence of that Promise; rather than one who despairs of obtaining Pardon. Let Luther then propose that no more for a Thing so new, and strange to us, which everybody already knows. Let him not any longer complain, that this is out of Use, then which nothing is more usual.

CHAPTER VII
Of Contrition

Having thus blotted out, (says Luther) the Promise and Faith; let us see what they have substituted in their Place. They allotted (says he) three Parts to Penance, Contrition, Confession, and Satisfaction/ All which three he so handles, that it appears well enough that none of them pleaseth him. First of all, he is very angry with Contrition, and calls the Anger of God in supportable; because Place is given to Attrition, and God is believed to supply, by the Sacrament, what is wanting to Man in the Sorrow for his Sins, when it is less vehement.

Let us see how well he maintains what he says; what he brings against himself. He teaches Contrition to be a great Thing, not easily had: He commands all Men to be certain that they have it; and to believe undoubtedly, that, through the Words of the Promise, all their Sins are forgiven them; and that after they are loosed by the Word of Man here on Earth, they are absolved by God in Heaven. In which Thing, his own Assertion will either fall back upon what he has already reprehended, or else will appear much more absurd.

For God has either promised to forgive Sins through Penance, to those only, who grieve as much for them as the Nature and Greatness of their Sins require, or to those who grieve not so much; or, finally, to such as are in no wise sorry for their Sins. If he has promised Forgiveness only to those, who are as contrite as the Greatness of their Crimes requires; then cannot Luther himself, (as he commands all others to be) be assured, and out of Doubt, that his Sins are forgiven him. For how will he be certain of his obtaining the Promise, when he can in no-wise know that he is sufficiently contrite for his Sins? For no mortal Man has ever yet known, how great Contrition is required for mortal Sin. If God has promised Pardon to such as are less contrite, then the Greatness of their Sins requires, then has he promised it to such as are called Attrites; and by that Luther agrees with those he but now reprehended. But if God has promised it to such as have no Manner of Sorrow for their Sins, he has surely much more promised it to such as are attrite, that is, to such as are in some Manner sorry. Wherefore if he admits but only Contrition, that is, a sufficient Grief, then can no Body be assured, that he is absolved; and Luther's certain and undoubted Confidence of Absolution, will perish, or be false, and erroneous.

But if he says, that the Sins of such as do only per form a slack, or luke-warm Penance, are not otherwise forgiven, then by the Sacrament of Penance; by confessing themselves Sinners, and asking and obtaining Pardon by the Mouth of their Brother: What is this different from the Opinion of those whom he reproves, who say, that Attrition, by Means of the Sacrament of Penance, is made Contrition? For what is wanting to Men, is supplied by the Sacrament; or else Luther's Position, that Man must be certain of Absolution, is false: Whether he will or no, he must admit, if not the Word Attrition, at least the Thing signified by it; which, if he grants, (as he will do, if he flies not from his own Opinion;) it is a very unseasonable Trifle of him to contend concerning the Word, and to allow the Effect. Again; he sets upon the whole Church with magnificent Words; as though it perversely taught Contrition, in exhorting us to acquire it by the Collection and Aspect of our Sins; when we ought to be first taught, as he says, the Beginnings and Causes of Contrition, to wit, the immoveable Truth of divine Threatenings and Promises ; as though such Things were not everywhere taught among the People; many Passages of Scripture for that Opinion being alleged, not less threatening, nor less comfortable; the Causes likewise added to procure Contrition; nor less efficacious, than those which Luther exacts and much more holy. For these Causes do almost propose Nothing, but the Fear of Punishment, or the Hopes of Reward; which is a Conversion not so acceptable to God, as a Conversion caused by Love. That may be done, not only by proposing what Luther advises, viz. God's Threatenings, and Promise of Remission; but also, what they teach, whom Luther derides; as if they taught Nothing at all, to wit, the Bounty of God towards us, and his exceeding great Benefits conferred upon us; when, not only undeserving Good, but even demeriting Evil. For the Sinner, having considered these Things, will rather be touched with Sorrow, for having offended so pious a Father, then so potent a Lord; and will less dread his own Punishment, than God's Anger: Neither will he be so desirous of Heaven, as of God's Favor: This Consideration of divine Bounty formeth Contrition; (Knowest thou, Man, says the Apostle, that the Bounty of God invites thee to Penance?[48]) and, as I have said,

---

[48] Rom. 2:4

forms a more holy Contrition, then that which, from the Fear of Punishment, and Hopes of Pardon, is formed by Luther; who boasts, that no Body teaches Threatenings but himself; when all Men do teach them, and better too.

CHAPTER VIII
Of Confession

He so treats of Confession, as to hold, that in public Crimes, where the Sin is known to all People, without Confession, there (where it is less Matter,) Confession is to be made. But, in the Confession of secret Sins, he has so uncertain Turnings, that, though he seem not altogether to reject it, yet can it not be known by him whether he admits it as a Thing commanded, or no: For he denies it to be proved by Scripture; and yet says, That it pleases him well, and that it is profitable and necessary; yet he does not say it to be necessary to all; but, as I suppose, only to pacify troubled Consciences; giving it to be understood, that if any Body have a Conscience like his own, which should be either safe for his own Sanctity, or assured of the Word of the

divine Promise; he need not confess his secret Sins at all, otherwise, if any Man be scrupulous, he may confess himself, to quiet his Conscience. Wherefore, seeing he has so dubiously suspended his Words, I have thought fit to speak something more plainly of the Necessity of Confession: And because he denies Confession of secret Sins to be proved by Scripture, I will, in the first Place, propose that Passage in Ecclesiasticus, which seems to many besides me, to comprehend all the three Parts of Penance. My Son, (saith he) neglect not thyself in thine Infirmity, but adore our Lord, and he will cure thee; Turn thyself from thy Sins, and lift up thine Hand, and cleanse thy Heart from all Sin[49]. For God cures, whilst he looses in Heaven what the Priest has loosed on Earth: We lift up our Hands in a Satisfaction; we turn from our Sins by Contrition; and in Confession, we cleanse our Hearts from Sin; according to that Saying of the Prophet, Pour out your Hearts before him[50]. St. Chrysostom also comprehends the three Parts of Penance, when he says, Perfect Penance compels the Sinner to endure all Things willingly; and further he says, Contrition in his Heart, Con fession in his Mouth, a perfect Humility in his Works; this is fruitful Penance. This also makes for Confession; Know the Face of your own Cattle: :(: But how can he know it, if it be not shewn him? What is clearer than that in Numbers the fifth, The Lord spoke to Moses, saying, speak to the Children of Israel, when a Man or Woman has committed a Sin, of all the Sins which are wont to happen unto Men; and have through Negligence, transgressed the Commandments of our Lord, and have sinned; they shall confess their Sins.

To this also belongs that of the Jewish old Law, which had all Things in Figure, the People infected with the Leprosy were commanded to shew themselves to the Priest. For if God has therefore written in the Law, You shall not bind the Mouth of the Oxen that treads out the Corn[51]; that he might admonish us, that it is but just, that he that serves at the Altar, should live by the Altar, (as the Apposttle declares, who says, that this is written in the Law, not for the Oxen, but for Men: For what Care, saith he, takes God for Oxen?[52])There is no Reason of Doubt, but that, by this Leprosy of the Body in the carnal Law, was signified that of Sin in the spiritual Law. And that Christ might bring us to the Understanding of this, by Degrees, he said to the Lepers which he cleansed, not only from the Leprosy of the Body, but also of the Soul; Go shew yourselves to the Priest. That of St. James also, confess your Sins to one another: Though I am not ignorant of the various Interpretations given by many to this Place; yet I am of Opinion, and many more besides me, that it is commanded of sacramental Confession. Or doth not that manifestly confirm Confession which our Lord saith by Esais, declare thou thy Wickedness that thou mayest be justified? If the Authority of the Fathers ought to have any Credit, sure it deserves it in this. St. Ambrose saith, No Man can be justified from Sin, if he do not confess his Sin. What can be more plainly spoken? Moreover, St. John Chrysostom says, He cannot receive the Grace of God, unless he be cleansed from all his Sins, by Confession. Lastly, St. Augustine, Do Penance, such as is done in the Church; Let no Man say to himself, I do it secretly, because I do it with God:

Therefore, without Reason was it said, what you shall loose on Earth[53]: Therefore, without Reason is it that the Keys were given. Put the Case, that not one Word was particularly, or figuratively read of Confession, nor any Thing spoken of it by the holy Fathers; yet, when I consider that all People have discovered their Sins to the Priests, for so many Ages; when I consider the Good that continually follows the Practice of it, and no Evil at all; I cannot think, or believe it to be established, or upheld by any

---

[49] Ecc. 38:9-10, Prov. 27:23
[50] Ps. 111:9, Num. 5:5-7
[51] Deut. 25:4; Jam. 5:16
[52] 1 Corn. 9:9, Is. 43:26, Lu. 27:14
[53] Matt. 18:18

human Invention, but by the divine Order of God. For the People could never, by any human Authority, be induced to discover their secret Sins, which they abhor in their Consciences, and which they are so much concerned to conceal, with such Shame, and Confusion, and so undoubtedly to a Man that might, when he pleased, betray them. Neither could it happen, that among such great Numbers of Priests, some good, and some bad, indifferently hearing Confessions, they should all retain them; and that also, when some of them can keep nothing else secret; if God himself, the Author of the Sacrament, did not, by his especial Grace, defend this so wholesome a Thing. For my Part, let Luther say what he will, I will believe that Confession was instituted, and is preserved by God himself; not by any Custom of the People, or Institution of the Fathers.

Now Luther s condemning the Reservation of some Sins, by which a particular Priest is restrained from remitting all; but that some are not forgiven, but by the Hand of a Bishop, some by the Hand of the Pope himself; This shews how this popular Man so levels all Things, as that, through the Hatred he bears to the chief Bishop, he casts all other Bishops into the Rank of the lowest Priest; being so blinded with Malice, as not to discern Jurisdiction, from Order; nay, so blind, as not to see any Order at all; but mingles and confounds all Things with Horror, and reduces Priests themselves into the Rank of Lay-men. Seeing that God has formed this his Church-militant to the Example of the triumphant; why, reading there so many Degrees, so many Orders, admits he in this neither Degree, nor Order, nor any Difference at all? Why then has the Apostle writ so much of Bishops, if a Bishop has no more Power over his Flock, than any other Priest, nor than a Lay-man? But we will speak of the Laity hereafter; let us now speak of Priests. Every Priest indeed has Orders, but not Authority of judging, any Thing belonging to him that absolves, before the Care of some Flock be committed unto him: Yet he is thought a fit Person for it before. If the Bishop then, who has Care of the whole Diocese, commits any Part of his Care to a Priest; does not Reason teach us, that this Man can bind or loose no more than what the other has permitted him, without whose Command, he could not have bound or loosed any Thing at all amongst the People? for the same Thing is not lawful for the Bishop to do in another Diocese. What Wonder then, if the Bishop reserves some Things to himself, whose Care is greater than what might be committed to every Person, though not the least learned, when it has been for so many Ages observed; fearing lest the People should fall more pronely into Sin, when the Power of Remission should be proposed to them in so easy a Manner? Luther now at last, that no Body, through the Difficulty of Penance, should be deterred from Sin, commands everything to be permitted to every Person; not to Priests only, but also to the Laity: Nay, he comes to that Height of Madness, that, though Women have commonly that bad Esteem of not being able to conceal any Thing of a Secret; yet is he willing Men should have them to hear their Confessions! But I suppose, since the Apostle permits not a Woman to teach, Luther will not make her a Priest; because he denies almost any to be a Priest, who is not a Preacher. But the Sentiments of the holy Fathers declare, that we ought to confess our Sins only to Priests, unless otherwise forced by Necessity: Let him come, (saith St. Augustin) to the Priests, who can administer to him the Keys of the Church. He does not say, let him come to Lay-men, or let him come to Women. The same Thing he further tells us more plainly, in another Place: He that repents, let him truly repent; let him signify his Grief by Tears; let him present his Life to God by the Priest; let him prevent the Judgment of God by Confession. For the Lord commanded them that should be cleansed, that they should shew themselves to the Priest: By this, teaching us, that Sins are to be confessed by a corporal Presence. Likewise, Pope Leo; Christ gave this Power to the Governors of the Church, that they should give the Satisfaction of Penance to them that confess. Further, venerable Bede; Let us discover our light and daily Crimes to our Co-equals, and our grievous Sins to the Priest; and as long as they have Dominion in us, let us take Care to purge them; for Sins cannot be forgiven, without Confession. Moreover, what should Confession avail us, if Absolution did not follow by the Keys of the Church: But this Power (saith St. Ambrose) is given only to Priests. In another Place, he declares what the Sense of these Words is, when he says, The Words of God remit Sin, the Priest is Judge. Likewise, St. Augustine, in another Place, writes most plainly, saying, He that doth Penance, without the Appointment of the Priest, frustrates the Keys of the Church. Now let any one judge of the Truth of Luther s Opinion, who, contrary to the Sentiments of all the holy Fathers, draws the Keys of the Church to the Laity, and to Women; and says, that these Words of Christ, whatsoever you shall bind, et cetera. are spoken not only to Priests, but also to all the Faithful. Marcus Aemilius Scaurus, a Man most excellent, and of known Honesty, being accused at Rome to the People, by Varius Sucronensis, a Man of little Sincerity; his Accuser having made a long and tedious Discourse; Scaurus confidently relying on the Judgment of the People, not thinking him worthy of an Answer, said, Romans, Varius Sucronensis says it, Aemilius Scaurus denies it; which of them do you believe? By which Words, the People, applauding this honorable Man, scorned the idle Accusations of his babbling Adversary. Which Discourse seems not more applicable to them, than to what we hear state: For Luther says, That the Words of Christ concerning the Keys are spoken to the Laity; St. Augustine denies it: Which of them is the rather to be believed? Luther affirms, Bede denies; which of them will you believe? Luther affirms, St. Ambrose denies; which of them has the greatest Credit? Finally, Luther affirms it, and the whole Church deny it: Which do you think is to be believed? But if any Body be so mad, as to believe with Luther, that he ought to confess himself to a Woman; perhaps it may not be amiss for him also to follow the other Opinion of Luther; in which he persuades us, not to be too careful in calling to Mind our Sins. For certainly, it is not altogether convenient to be too solicitous in examining your Memory for what you are to put into such a Person's Ear, who has so large and passable a Road from her Ear to her Tongue. Otherwise seeing it may be done without any such Danger; I shall not scruple to prefer, before the Council of Luther, the Example of the Prophet; who saith, In Bitterness will I reckon over all my Years unto thee[54]; all my Years, (says he) and that in Bitterness: For such a Confession, not only cleanses from Sins past, but also begets abundantly new Grace; according to that of St. Ambrose, St. Peter became more faithful after he bewailed the Loss of his Faith; and so he obtained a greater Grace than he had lost/ St. Gregory, following him, says, That Life, which is fervent in Love after Sin, is much more acceptable to God, then Innocence that is sluggish in Security. When Luther calls them idle People, who are of Opinion that the Circumstances of Sin are to be con fessed; see how much in this St. Augustine differs from him, when he says, let him consider the Quality of the Crime; as to the Place, Time, Perseverance, Distinction of Persons, and with what Temptation it was done, how often the Sin was committed?

---

[54] Is. 38:15

For a Fornicator ought to repent according to the Excellency of his State, or Affairs, and according to the Quality of the Person with whom he has sinned; according to the Crime itself; if in a sacred Place, in Time of Prayer, as holy Days, and Times of fasting; he is to consider how long he persisted in Sin, and let his Sorrow be according to his Perseverance in Sin, and by what Assault he was overcome; for some there are, who, far from being overcome, do voluntarily offer themselves to Sin; nor do they stay for Temptation, but prevent the Pleasure: Let him consider with what Pleasure, and how often, he has committed the Sin: All these Circumstances are to be confessed, and bewailed; that when he has known his Sin, he may soon find God propitious to him. In pondering the Weight of his Offences, let him consider of what Age he is, of what Understanding, and Order: Let him ponder each of these singly, and examine the Manner of the Crime, purging with Tears every Quality of the Vice. Hitherto the Words of St. Augustine: That Luther may not think that Circumstances do not appertain to Confession; who has more diligently reckoned up the Circumstances of Sins, then this Holy Man? I scarce know whether Luther will find any one of these he calls idle. But, if the various Circumstances of Sin are so diligently to be called to Mind, how much more are heinous and different Crimes to be collected, and our Conscience diligently to be examined, that, if possible, we may not let one Sin escape our Knowledge? For what Luther darts as a keen Shaft, that no Body can possibly confess all his Sins, because none can remember them all, is indeed but a very obtuse one: For who knows not, that none of those who said, all Sins are to be confessed, was so stupid as to think that a Man must tell the Priest in his Ear, what came not into his own Memory to confess?

CHAPTER IX
Of Satisfaction

I know not how Luther will satisfy others concerning Satisfaction: For my Part, I think that, rather than he would remain silent, he would choose to speak many Things of no Signification at all. For first, when he says, That the Church so teaches Satisfaction, as that the People can never understand true Satisfaction, which is a Renovation of Life; who does not see it to be a Calumny? Who taught Luther, that the Church does not teach, that we ought to renew our Lives? He has not travelled over the whole Church; he has not been present at all Confessions, to hear this Ignorance of the Priests: He must then have the holy Ghost in his Bosom, or some Devil in his Breast, who has inspired this into him. But what Spirit soever this was, it could not be a good one, that taught him a Lye, but that Spirit, of whom it is said, The Devil is a Liar, and the Father of Lies[55]; for there is none that knows not that to be false, which Luther affirms to be true: For who was ever so doltish, as to enjoin such satisfactory Works for past Sins, as should indulge the future? Who does not continually, when he absolves, pronounce these Words of Christ, Go, and sin no more? And that of St. Paul, as you have exhibited

---

your Members to serve Uncleanness, and Iniquity, unto Iniquity, so now exhibit your Members to serve Justice unto Sanctification. Who has not read that of St. Gregory, we are not able to perform our Penance, as we ought, unless we know the Manner of the same Penance? For to do Penance, is to bewail our Sins formerly committed, and resolve not to do any Thing hereafter that we should have cause to sorrow for. For he that laments the past, so as to commit the future, knows not how to perform Penance, but dissembleth. What avails it to any Body, to grieve for his Sins of Luxury, and yet to burn with Covetousness? If there were Nothing of this said; yet seeing the Priest imposes Penance for Sins committed, he shews that the Thing itself is not to be again committed, which must again be punished. It is therefore very evident, that Luther has no Regard to what he says, so he may but say Somewhat that may slander the Church: Which Thing always appears wheresoever, (as in some Matter of great Moment) he cries aloud, even as he does in these Words: For what monstrous Things are we indebted to thee, thou See of Rome! and to thy murthering Laws and Rites, whereby thou hast so destroyed the whole World, that People think they can satisfy God for their Sins, by Works; when Nothing, but the Faith only of a contrite Heart, can satisfy; which, by these Tumults, thou not only puttest to Silence, but even oppressest, only that thy insatiable Blood-suckers may have People to say to them, bring, bring, that you may sell Sins P Who would not think, by reading these so furious and tragical Words, but Luther had discovered some great, and abominable Prodigies in the Roman See? But he that diligently examines all these Things, will see that the Mountains bring forth a ridiculous Mouse: For first, how ridiculous is that Exclamation of his against the See of Rome? As if Works of Satisfaction were only exacted, and Penance imposed only at Rome, and not through the whole Church, in all Parts of the World; or, as if many of the Laws, which he calls murthering Laws, were not ordained in former Times by the holy Fathers, and public Consent of all Christians, in Synods, and general Councils. Finally, when he says, that we cannot satisfy God by Works, but by Faith alone; if he means, that by Works alone, without Faith, we cannot do it; he shews but his Folly, by railing against the See of Rome; in which none was ever yet so foolish, as to say, that Works, without Faith, can satisfy; being not ignorant of that of St. Paul, what is not of Faith is Sin[56]. But if he thinks that Works are superfluous, and that Faith alone is sufficient, whatever the Works be; then he says Something, and dissents truly from the Roman Church; which, with St. James, believes, That Faith, without Works, is dead. You see how impertinently Luther troubles himself, who so furiously inveighs against the Roman See, as in the mean While thus to involve himself in the Snares of Folly and Impiety. Although indeed, I think it is more probable, that Luther is of Opinion, that Faith without good Works, is always sufficient to Salvation: For, that he is of that Opinion, evidently appears; as well by other Passages of his, as by his saying, That God does Nothing regard our Works, nor has any Need of them: But he has Need that we should esteem him true in his Promises. What Luther meant by these Words, he knows best himself. For my Part, I believe, that God cares for our Faith and our Works, and that he stands in Need of neither our Faith, nor our Works. For though God has no Want of our Goods, yet has he so much Care of what we do, that he commands some Things to be done, and forbids other Things: Without whose Care, not so much as one Sparrow falls to the Earth, five of which are sold for two Farthings. But because Luther

---

[56] Rom. 15:23, Jam. 2:17-20, Lu. 12:6

urges that a Penitent ought only to renew his Life, and neglect to undergo any Penance from the Priest, for his past Sins; let us hear what St. Augustine has writ on this Subject: It is not sufficient (says he) to change our Manners to better, and forsake our former Wickedness; unless we do also satisfy our Lord, for the Sins committed, by the Sorrow of Penance, by the Sobs of Humility; by the Sacrifice of a contrite Heart, with the Co-operation of Alms-deeds, and Fasts. And in another Place, he saith, Let the Penitent deliver himself altogether unto the Judgment and Power of the Priest; reserving Nothing of himself to himself, that he may be ready to do all Things, as he is commanded, towards recovering the Life of the Soul; which he should do, to avoid the Death of the Body. Likewise, in another Place, The Priests do also bind, (says he) while they enjoin the Satisfaction of Penance to those who come to Confession; they lose when they remit any Thing thereof: For they exercise a Work of Justice towards Sinners, when they bind them with just Punishment; a Work of Mercy, when they remit Somewhat of the same Punishment: I hope I have plainly made appear how rashly he calumniates the Church; and through the whole Sacrament of Penance, how impertinent, how impious, and how absurd he is against the holy Fathers; against Scriptures; against the public Faith of the Church; against the Consent of so many Ages and People; even against Common-sense itself; with all which, he is not yet content; but, after having held a long Time that Penance is a Sacrament, he began, in the End of his Book, to repent himself, that it should contain any Thing of Truth at all; and therefore, as his Custom is, changes his Opinion into a worse, and wholly denies Penance to be a Sacrament. Yet he confesses before, that he does not doubt, but that whoever, of his own Accord, or moved by Reproofs, has privately confessed himself before any Brother, and demanded Pardon, and amends himself, is absolved from all his secret Sins. If that be his Sentiment, though false indeed; (because he says, before any Brother privately, and that indifferently; whether he ask Pardon of his own Accord, or as forced thereto by Rebukes:) If, I say, he thinks such a Penance to be profitable, why excludes he it from the Number of the Sacraments? not indeed, for any other Intent, but that it may be the less valued; and, being deprived of the Name of a Sacrament, (which amongst Christians is in great Veneration) it might become despicable: For which Thing he finds no other Pretext, but that Penance has no visible Sign; as though the exterior Penance, or the very Act and Gestures of the Body, when the Priest absolves the Penitent, could not be a Sign of spiritual Grace, by which the Penitent obtains Remission. But, in fine, to conclude the Discourse of Penance, I wish he may at last repent himself, for having treated of Penance after so evil a Manner; that he may wholesomely perform all its Parts, as he endeavors to destroy them all; that he may be contrite for his Malice, confess publicly his Errors; and that, submitting himself to the Judgment of the Church, (which with so many Blasphemies he has offended) he may recompense for what he has before committed, with the greatest Satisfaction possible; for indeed he cannot do it worthily.

CHAPTER X
Of Confirmation

Luther is so far from admitting Confirmation to be a Sacrament, that, on the Contrary, he says, he admires what the Church's Intention was in making it one. And this most impertinent Babbler trifles thus in so sacred a Thing; asking why the Church does not make three Sacraments of Bread, as having in Scripture some Occasions to do it? The Church has not done any such Thing, because she takes no Occasions, from any Words whatsoever in Scripture, for having any other Sacraments, then those which were instituted by Christ, and sanctified by his most holy Blood: Even so it omits none of them which have been given by Christ and his Apostles, and transmitted to us, as it were, from Hand to hand, though Nothing should be writ of them in any Place.

But when he says, that Confirmation works no Salvation, and that it is supported by no Promise of Christ; he only says this, proving Nothing, but only denying all. But when Luther makes Mention of some Passages, from which (though he laughed at it) the Sacrament of Confirmation may probably have its Beginning; why judges he so perversely of the whole Church, as if it should rashly admit a Sacrament; because he reads no Word of Promise in these Places; as if Christ had promised, said, or done Nothing, but what the Evangelists mention in the Scriptures! By this Rule, if there was no Gospel but that of St. John, he should deny the Institution of the Sacrament of our Lord's Supper; of which Institution St. John writes Nothing at all: Many other Things done by Jesus have been omitted by all; which (as the Evangelist himself saith) are not written in this Book, and which the whole World could not contain[57]; of which, some have, by the Mouth of the Apostles, been delivered to the Faithful, and have been ever after conserved by the perpetual Faith of the holy Catholic Church; whom, I think, you ought to believe concerning some Things which are not in the Gospels; when, (as St. Augustine says) You could never know which is the Scripture itself, but by the Tradition of the Church. And though none should have been ever written, yet the Gospel would have always remained written in the Hearts of the Faithful, which was more ancient than all the Books of the Evangelists. Let not Luther think it is a prevailing Argument to prove the Nullity of the Sacraments, not to find them instituted in the Scriptures. Otherwise, if he admits Nothing at all, but what he reads clearly in the Gospel, (that he may have no Place for Wrangling) how comes he to believe, (if he believes it, for he scarce believes any Thing at all) the perpetual Virginity of the blessed Virgin Mary? Of which he is so far from finding any Thing in Scripture, that Helvidius took Occasion by Scripture itself to prove the Contrary. Neither is any Thing opposed against him, but the Faith of the whole Church, which is nowhere greater and stronger than in the Sacraments. For my Part, I do not think that any Person, who has the least Spark of Faith in him, can be persuaded, that Christ, who prayed for St. Peter, that his Faith should not fail[58]; who placed his Church on a firm Rock; should suffer her, for so many Ages, to be bound by vain Signs of corporal Things, under an erroneous Confidence of their being divine Sacraments. If Nothing should be read of it anywhere, yet those who were present, and conversed with our Lord, could, by Word of Mouth,

---

[57] Jn. 21:25
[58] Lu. 22:32

tell what his Mind was, of whom himself says, Ye are Witnesses who have been with me from the Beginning[59] What was to be done, might be taught by the Holy Ghost, of whom Christ said, But when the Paraclete comes, whom I will send you from the Father, the Spirit of Truth which proceedeth from the Father, he[60] shall give Testimony of me[61]. And in another Place, when lie shall come, that is, the Spirit of Truth, he shall teach you all Truth, for he shall not speak of himself; but what Things soever he shall hear, he shall speak; and the Things that are to come he shall shew you. Shall we believe then, that the Church, having so many, and so great Ministers, so many living Evangelists, and that Spirit which inspires Truth, has rashly instituted a Sacrament, and puts her Hope in an empty Sign? Or shall we not rather believe, that it has learned from the Apostles, and from the Spirit of Truth? Certainly, if the Name of this Sacrament, the Minister, and the Virtue promised in it, be considered, it will appear not to be a Thing which we may believe to be unadvisedly used by the Church. For, as Hugo de St. Victore saith, From Chrism is Christ named; from Christ, Christian; everyone ought to have taken Chrism, or Unction, since from it they take their common Name. For we are all an elected Nation, and a royal Priesthood in Christ: We are not anointed, unless in Case of Necessity, but by the Bishops, that they may seal the Christian, and give him the Holy Ghost: Even (says he) as we read that the Apostles only, in the primitive Church, had Power to give the Holy Ghost by Imposition of Hands. The same Doctor declares also the Fruit of the Sacrament; As the Remission of Sins, (saith he) is received in Baptism; so, by the Imposition of Hands, the Holy Ghost is given: There, Grace is given to the Remission of Sins: Here, Grace is given to Confirmation; for what avails it you to be lifted up from your Fall, if you are not confirmed to stand? These are Hugo's Words, which are also consonant to Reason. For as in the corporal Life, besides Generation, by which we get Life, another Action is required, by which we may increase, and grow to the Perfection of Strength: So, in the spiritual Life, which is required by Regeneration in Baptism, the Sacrament of Confirmation is necessary, by which the spiritual Life is led to perfect Virtue, and the Holy Ghost is given for perfect Strength. And besides, the Sacrament of Baptism, which helps us to believe, Confirmation is profitable to give us Courage to confess our Faith boldly. For to this it is ordained, that Man may, before the Persecutor, boldly confess his Faith: And this is what Melchiades saith; In Baptism we are regenerated to Life, after Baptism we are confirmed for the Combat; for Confirmation arms and in structs us against the Agonies of this World.

Finally, that Luther may understand that this Sacrament is no new Thing, or vain Fiction; but that it is so far from being void of Grace, that it confers the Spirit of Grace and Truth: We will here relate what St. Jerome has written of this Sacrament of Confirmation. If the Bishop impose his Hand, it is on them who have been baptized in the true Faith, who have believed in the Father, Son, and Holy Ghost, three Persons

---

[59] Jn. 15:27

[60] Jn. 16:13

[61] Jn. 15:26, 1 Pet. 2:9

and one Substance. But the Arian, who believes in no other (stop your Ears, that you may not be polluted with the Words of such monstrous Impiety,) but in the Father alone, in Jesus Christ as a Creature, in the Holy Ghost as Servant to both; how shall he receive the Holy Ghost from the Church, who has not as yet obtained Remission of his Sins? For the Holy Ghost inhabits not, but where Faith is pure, nor remains but in that Church which has true Faith for her Guide.

If in this Place, you ask why he that is baptized in the Church, receives not the Holy Ghost but by the Hands of the Bishop? Learn, that this Observation is descended from this Authority; because, after our Lord's Ascension, the Holy Ghost descended on the Apostles, and we find the same to have been done in many Places. Hitherto St. Jerome. Which Sentence is also confirmed by divers Passages in the Scripture, and particularly by that in the Acts, which shews that the People baptized before in Samaria, received the Holy Ghost, when Peter and John came among them, and laid their Hands upon them[62]. I therefore admire how it should come into Luther's Mind to dispute, that Confirmation is only to be accounted a Rite and a Ceremony, and deny it to be a Sacrament; when it is demonstrated, not only by the Testimony of holy Fathers, and by the Faith of the whole Church, but also by clear Passages of Scripture; that not only Grace, but also, the very Spirit of Grace, is conferred by the visible Sign of the Bishop's Imposition of Hands.

Let Luther therefore forbear to contemn any more the Sacrament of Confirmation, which the Dignity of the Minister, the Authority of the Church, and the Profit of the Sacrament itself, commend.

---

[62] Act. 8:14-17

CHAPTER XI
Of the Sacrament of Marriage

Marriage, the first of all Sacraments, celebrated by the first of Mankind, and honored with our Savior's first Miracle, being for so long Time had in a religious Veneration for its very Name of a Sacrament; is now, at last, (that People should not so much regard or value conjugal Faith,) denied by Luther to be any Sacrament at all; and as in other Sacraments, (some of which he takes away, by denying the Sign instituted; others, by denying promised Grace) he denies both of them to be in Marriage; (holding, that Grace has been no where promised thereby) he teaches also, that it has been nowhere instituted for a Sign: And how knows he this? Because (says he) we read it not. O strong Reason, and Mother of many Heresies! This was the Fountain, from which Helvidius drew his Venom. You admit no Sacrament, unless you read its Institution in a Book! What Book has he ever writ who instituted all? Concerning some Things, (says he) I believe Christ s Evangelists: Why then does he not, in some Things, believe also the Church of Christ; which is by Christ himself preferred to all the Evangelists, who have been only Members of the Church? Wherefore, if he confides so much in one, why does he distrust all together? If he attributes so much to a Member, why nothing at all to the whole Body?

The Church believes it to be a Sacrament; that it has been instituted by God; given by Christ; and left to us by his Apostles; delivered afterwards by the Holy Fathers for a Sacrament, and given as it were, from Hand to Hand down to us; from us also, as a

Sacrament, down to Posterity, and to be honored to the End of the World. The Church believes this; and tells you what it believes too. The same Church that says, The Evangelists writ the Gospel, tells you this also. For if the Church had not said, That the Gospel of John, is the Gospel of John, you should not have known it; for you were not present when he writ it. Why then do you not believe the Church, when she tells you that Christ has done these Things; has instituted these Sacraments; that the Apostles have delivered them; as well as when she says, That the Evangelists writ such, and such Gospels?

But Luther says, Marriage was amongst the ancient Patriarchs, and amongst the Gentiles; and that as truly as amongst us, yet was it not a Sacrament with either of them. As for the Fathers that were under the Law, and before the Law, I do not agree with Luther; but am certain, that Marriage was a Sacrament with them as well as Circumcision. But amongst the Gentiles, the Case is otherwise; for their Marriage depended on the Custom and Laws of each People: So that some Marriages were lawful with some of them, which by others were accounted ridiculous: And yet, contrary to Luther, we find some of Opinion, that even the Marriages of the Gentiles were a Sacrament amongst them. For St. Augustine says, That the Sacrament of Marriage is common to all Nations: But the Sanctity of it is only in the City of our God, and in his holy Mountain (the Church.) On which Sentiment, let him that pleases read Hugo de Sancto Victore. But though the Marriage of the Unfaithful be no Sacrament, yet does it not follow what Luther infers, That the Marriage of the Faithful is none either. For the People of God have something more holy in Marriage, and have always had, as well as its first Institution, as when it was honored with Laws given by God. Moreover, the Gentiles, because it was acted as a human Thing amongst them, were wont, by Compacts and human Laws, to take Wives, and after to reject them again. Divorcement was not lawful in former Times amongst the People of God: For though God, by Moses, permitted the Bill of Divorcement among the Hebrews; yet Christ confesses that it was indulged them for the Hardness of the People's Hearts: For, from the Beginning (saith our Savior,) it was not so. But Christ hath restored Christians to pristine Sanctity, consecrating Marriage with an indesolvable Bond of Society; unless in Case of Fornication between those, whom no human Error, but God himself, has joined together. It follows not, therefore, that if Marriage has not been a Sacrament amongst the Gentiles, it must be none amongst us Christians, or has not been a Sacrament amongst the ancient Patriarchs; amongst Christians, if it was nowhere read, yet the Faith of the Church ought to suffice us. And yet that one Passage of the Apostle, which Luther endeavors to put by with a Scoff, does plainly demonstrate, that Marriage, not only now, but also at the very first Beginning of Mankind, was instituted a Sacrament: Which I suppose will not be doubted by any Body who reads that Part of the Epistle to the Ephesians, and attentively considers it. Which whole Passage we have here inserted; because, by any Man's Words, it cannot be more clearly explicated, than it is already by the Apostle himself, who has so plainly shewn us his Mind therein, that no Place of Refuge is left to Luther s impertinent Calumnies. For he saith, Let Women be subject to their Husbands, as to our Lord: Because the Man is Head of the Woman, as Christ is Head of the

Church: Himself the Savior of his Body. But as the Church is subject to Christ, so the Women to their Husbands, in all Things. Husbands love your Wives, even as Christ loved the Church, and delivered himself for it. That he might sanctify it, cleansing it by the Laver of Water in the Word; That he might present to himself a glorious Church, not having Spot or Wrinkle, or any such Thing; but that it may be holy and unspotted. So also, Men ought to love their Wives as their own Bodies; he that loveth his Wife, loveth himself. For no Man ever hated his own Flesh, but he nourishes it and cherishes it, as also Christ the Church; because we are Members of his Body, of his Flesh, and of his Bones: For this Cause shall a Man leave Father and Mother, and cleave to his Wife, and they shall be two in one Flesh; This is a great Sacrament: But I speak in Christ, and in the Church[63]. You see how the blessed Apostle teacheth every-where, that the Marriage of Man and Wife is a Sacrament, which represents the Conjunction of Christ with his Church: For he teacheth, that God consecrated Matrimony, that it might be the Mystery of Christ joined with his Church. He tells you, That the Man and Wife make one Body, of which the Man is the Head; and that Christ and the Church make one Body, of which Christ is the Head. He makes the chief Cause why the Husband ought to love his Wife, no other, then that he may not be an unlike Sign to Christ, whom he represents: And this he makes rather the Cause, than that common Nature of the Male and Female, which of itself should also excite Love. He, by the same Example, exhorts the Wife to fear and respect her Husband; that is, because she represents the Church of Christ. And after he has by many Words inculcated these Things over and over again; (fearing lest any Body should think this Comparison of the Husband with Christ, and the Wife with the Church, to be some Similitude, used only for the Conveniency of the Exhortation,) he shews it to be a true Matter, a true Sacrament, foretold by the Prophesy of the chiefest and first of all Prophets, when the World was but newly created: For when the Apostle saith, He that loves his Wife, loves himself; for no Man ever hated his own Flesh, but loves and cherishes it, even as Christ loveth his Church; because, (says he) we are Members of his Body, of his Flesh, and of his Bones. This he spoke to remind us of the Words, much like to these, which Adam spoke, when Eve was first brought into his Sight, this is Bone of my Bone, and Flesh of my Flesh.

And that the Apostle might more clearly shew that the Sacrament of the Conjunction of Adam and Eve pertains to that Union of Christ with his Church, he added Adam s very Words, wherefore a Man shall leave Father and Mother, and cleave to his Wife; and they shall be two in one Flesh[64].This Sacrament, saith the Apostle, is great in Christ and the Church. How could he have more evidently refuted Luther, than by these Words, which he so impertinently scoffs at, in contending that the Apostle had taken away the Sacrament from the Marriage of Man and Wife, by saying, This Sacrament is great in Christ and his Church? As if he should, by saying, the Sacrament of Baptism is great in the washing of the Soul, deny the Baptism of the Body to be a Sacrament; or, as if he should, by saying, the Sacrament of the Eucharist is great in the Body of Christ, deny the Species of Bread and Wine to be a Sacrament; or, as if by saying, That the same Sacrament is great in the mystical Body of Christ, he should detract the Sacrament from the Body which he took of the blessed Virgin. Who has ever seen any Man swell

---

[63] Eph. 5:22

[64] Gen. 2:23

with greater Pride for so frivolous a Gloss? For if the Apostle had been of his Opinion, and willing his Words should be so interpreted, as to shew this Sacrament to be great only in Christ and his Church, without any Reference at all to the Marriage of Man and Wife; it would lessen the Force and Weight of all those Things, where by, in that Comparison of the two Conjunctions, he had before commended Marriage.

It would also, in another Manner prejudice the Matter he undertook, if he should refer these Words of Adam only to Christ and his Church, which, of themselves, seem to unite Man and Wife together in mutual Love, so as to teach, that there is in them no Reference to Man and Wife. The Apostle teaches, that those Words of Adam, were a Prophecy of Christ and his Church; which is confirmed by all the holy Doctors, and very clearly demonstrated by Adam s speaking these Words at the very first Sight of Eve, by which he preferred a Wife to Father and Mother; nor as yet any Command of begetting Children, to instruct him, by the Comparison of Parents and Children, what Father and Mother were. Because, if those Words of Adam were a Prophecy of Christ and his Church, then it seems they either did not belong to that Marriage which was there performed; or that some Marriage, as a proper Sign of this Conjunction, was then made a Sacrament by God himself, whose Spirit then formed the Words of Adam, that the same Words might signify what was then done, and what was prophesied; that is, the Marriage of Men, and the Conjunction of Christ with the Church; and as one Sacrament comprehends a sacred Thing, and the proper and sacred Sign of the same thing.

Moreover, that you may the more plainly discern, that what Luther speaks, is to no Purpose; observe, that the Apostle's Business, in that Place, to the Ephesians, is not about teaching them how great a Sacrament Christ joined with the Church, is; but about exhorting married People how to behave themselves one towards another, so as they might render their Marriage a Sacrament, like, and agreeable to, that so sacred a Thing, of which it is the Sacrament. Luther., therefore, in this Place, is either negligent himself, and unadvisedly reads this Passage, or else he most impiously dissembles what Truth he discovers therein; when he says, that which we give, (which is the Sense of the whole Church) proceeds from great Idleness, Negligence and inconsiderate Reading thereof. Does St. Augustine therefore carelessly read the Apostle? Has St. Jerome negligently understood him? and all Men except Luther, by whose Vigilance St. Paul himself is discovered to have writ, not a Sacrament, but a Mystery? O this quick-sighted Man! who is able to see that the whole Latin Church does wrongfully name that a Sacrament, which the Apostle, writing in Greek, calls Mystery, and not Sacrament! as though the Latins had erred by speaking the Word in Latin, because St. Paul does not use a Latin Word in the Greek Tongue. If the Interpreter had translated it not a Sacrament, but a Mystery, and had left the Greek Word entire; yet had not this taken away the Argument, whereby Marriage is, from this Place of the Apostle, concluded to be a Sacrament; seeing it is taught so to be, by the Circumstance of the whole Matter. For let him wrest the Word Mystery, as much as he will; yet can he never by it take away, or deny, the Sacrament, though thereby it may not be proved. Neither shall it be said, that he speaks or thinks ill, who says, that the Eucharist is a great Mystery; for there is no Sacrament but what is a Mystery, that is, what contains, under a visible Sign, a secret and invisible Grace; the Interpreter noting in the Words of St. Paul to the Ephesians, that the whole Passage does most evidently declare the Apostle to write of such a Mystery as is a

Sacrament. And if he had not truly translated it, St. Augustine and St. Jerome, his Readers, were not so careless, but they would have discovered the Errors in the Translation: or were they so much inclined to favor Marriage, as to follow an Error, rather than correct it, when once discovered; especially, seeing St. Augustine was nothing inferior to Luther, in the Knowledge of the Greek Tongue: And St. Jerome, who, without Doubt, was the most skilled of his Time in that Language, did so favor Virginity, that, by some Persons, he was thought to be almost unjust towards Marriage.

Wherefore, that all Men may the more easily understand, not only these, whom Luther in Contempt calls sententious, and now idle Readers; but also, the best and most learned of the ancient Fathers of the Church; let us here what St. Augustine says, not only Fecundity, (says he) whose Fruit is in the Off-spring; not only in Chastity, whose Bond is Faith. but also, the Sacrament of Marriage, is commended to the Faithful, married People: For which Reason, the Apostle says, Husbands love your Wives, even as Christ loved his Church[65]: St. Augustine, then, calls it a Sacrament; and that Luther may not say he has read this Passage carelessly, he treats of the same Text, again and again, in divers Works. For in another Place, he says, it has been said in Paradise, Man shall leave Father and Mother, and cleave to his Wife[66]; which by the Apostle is called a great Sacrament in Christ and his Church.

Why does not St. Augustine explicate that Mystery of Luther to be an Error, which the Latins call a Sacrament; seeing that in the Greek Text St. Paul calls it Mystery, not Sacrament? St. Augustine, above a thousand Times, calls it the Sacrament of Marriage; as in that Place where he says, That Off-spring, Faith, and Sacrament, which are all the Goodness of Marriage, is fulfilled in the Parents, of Christ himself. Why has he not here admonished us, that it is not a Sacrament, but a Mystery? For if what Luther says, be true, to wit, that it is not a Sacrament, but concern Christ and his Church; then is it not true which St. Augustine says: For that which Luther takes for only a Mystery, is not the good Sacrament of Marriage, nor has it been fulfilled in the Marriage of the Virgin Mary.

And in another Place, St. Augustine, treating of the same Words of the Apostle, says, what is great in Christ and the Church, is very little in Man and Wife; and yet it is an inseparable Sacrament of Conjunction.

If Luther holds that it is not called a Sacrament, unless in Christ and his Church; the Apostle s very Words, if diligently examined only by a Grammarian, shall convince him; as when the Apostle says, This Sacrament is great; but I say in Christ and the Church. What Sacrament is that, that is great in Christ and the Church? Christ and the Church cannot be a Sacrament in Christ and the Church: For none speaks after this Manner. It is therefore a necessary Consequence, that this Sacrament, which he says is great in Christ and the Church, is that Conjunction of Man and Wife which he has spoken of. There is ^Nothing else but this spoken here by the Apostle, viz. This Conjunction of Man and Woman, is a great Sacrament in Christ and the Church, as a sacred Sign in a

---

[65] Eph. 5:25
[66] Gen. 2:24

most sacred Thing. Lastly, if Luther still obstinately deny, that (by these Words of the Apostle) Marriage should be called a Sacrament; but merely the Conjunction of Christ with the Church: Yet surely, he will not deny Conjunction of Man and Wife to be at least a Sign of that sacred Conjunction of Christ and his Church, and that too by God s own Institution; not by human Invention, seeing our first Parents were joined by God himself. But if he denies all this that has been said; the Apostle's Words will, however, manifest his Impudence: For it is so often, and so plainly repeated, that he who should not see it, must undoubtedly confess himself to be blind.

If therefore it shall evidently appear, that Grace is conferred by Marriage, which is a Sign of so sacred a Thing; Luther will be compelled, whether he will or no, to admit Marriage as a Sacrament, or else to reject all Sacraments; seeing that, by his own Confession, a Sacrament consists in the Sign of a sacred Thing, and the Promise of Grace. Let us see then, if it can be evidently made out, that Grace is infused after any Manner by Marriage; for Luther flatly denies it.

We read in no Place, (says he) that he who marries a Wife shall receive any Grace from God. Marriage (says the Apostle) is honorable in all, and a Bed undefiled[67]: The Bed could not be undefiled, if the Marriage wanted Grace; neither has Marriage any Thing else to confer, but a Bed unspotted. But because God, whose Bounty has provided, that no necessary Thing should be wanting, even to irrational Creatures, according to their several Natures and Capacities; nay, even to Things wanting Sense; has, by the like bountiful Providence, joined Grace to Marriage, by which, he that does not slight it, but keeps his Faith inviolate to his Wife, shall not only not contract any Blemish by the carnal Act, (whose filthy Concupiscence would otherwise stain him) but shall, on the Contrary, be advanced to Grace. For Marriage should not have an immaculate Bed, if the Grace, which is infused by it, did not turn that unto Good, which should be otherwise a Sin. Which, in another Passage of St. Paul, where he treats of the Woman's Duty, is more plainly demonstrated; She (saith he) shall be saved, through the Generation of Children[68]: But if you take away Marriage, what else shall Generation be, (by which, as the Apostle saith, there is no Salvation in Marriage) but Death and eternal Damnation? For, take away Marriage, (says St. Bernard) and an undefiled Bed from the Church, and do you not then fill it with Adulteries, Incests, Sodomy, and all Sorts of Uncleanness? If all Generation, out of Wedlock, is damnable, the Grace of Marriage must needs be great, by which that Act, (which of its own Nature defiles to Punishment) is not only purged, to take away the Blemish; but is so much sanctified, that, as the Apostle testifies, it becomes meritorious. Neither has it that Privilege of Grace, but by Virtue of the Sacrament, consecrated for that Purpose by God himself; that Man, at his first Creation, might, by the Use there of, both perform his Duty of Propagation, and have also a Remedy of Concupiscence, when restored: Yet what should the conjugal Act itself be, but Concupiscence, if God had not made it the Remedy thereof? Which now the holy Grace of the Sacrament has so made a Remedy of Concupiscence, as that the paternal Substance may not be negligently consumed, (as the prodigal Son had done) forbidding not only, not to thirst after stolen Waters of

---

[67] Heb. 13:4
[68] 1 Tim. 2:15

other Men's Cisterns, but also not to inebriate ourselves with our own; but make our sober Draughts so wholesome, that they may profit to Life everlasting. The Apostle, in the same Place, though he exhorted as much as possible to Continency and Virginity, (Virtues contrary to conjugal Generation) yet confesses, that Marriage is the Gift of God; and one of those Gifts, of which it is said, every good and perfect Gift is from above, descending from the Father of Lights[69]. And certainly, the Gift of God, (which is so given, that he who receives it, may continue in that State of Life, in which he ought to remain, and not fall into the State of Destruction) doth it not shew that it hath in itself preservative Grace?

Moreover, when the Apostle saith, if any Brother have a Wife, an Infidel, and she consent to live with him, let him not put her away: And if any Woman have an Husband, an Infidel, and he consent to dwell with her, let her not put away her Husband: For the Man, an Infidel, is sanctified by the faithful Woman; and the Woman, an Infidel, is sanctified by the faithful Hus
band; otherwise, your Children should be unclean; but now they are holy[70]. Do not these Words of the Apostle shew, that, in Marriage (which is an entire Thing of itself, after one of the Parties is converted to the Faith) the Sanctity of the Sacrament sanctifies the whole Marriage, which before was altogether unclean? But why should that Marriage be now more holy than before, (as being a Marriage) if, for one of the Parties converted, sacramental Grace were not added to it, which, before Baptism, (the Door of all the Sacraments) could not enter to the Marriage of the Unfaithful?

But, to pass by the Apostle; let us consider God, the Consecrator of this Sacrament. Has he not consecrated Marriage with his Blessing, when he joined together our first Parents? For the Scripture saith, God blessed them; saying, increase, and multiply[71]: Whose Blessing, having operated in all other living Creatures, according to their several Capacities; who should doubt but that he has infused the Force of spiritual Grace into the Spirit of Man, who alone is capable of Reason, unless he did believe, that God, (being so bountiful to the meanest of Beasts, as to give them largely, according to their Natures, what was necessary) should be so sparing of his Blessings to Man, whom he created after his own Image; that having only Regard to his Body, he should omit the Soul, that Breath of Life, which he himself has breathed, and by which he was most represented, without imparting any Part of that great Blessing to it?

Further; when Christ, God and Man, conversing amongst Men, not only honored Marriage with his own Presence, but also adorned it with his first Miracle; has he not taught, That Marriage is to be honored? And without Grace, I do not find any Thing in it deserving Honor. Nor do I think he would have been present at it, if Marriage had not already some Grace, which might render it acceptable to Christ; or else he conferred Grace to it himself: But I see, the Miracle that he wrought[72], admonishes us that the insipid Water of carnal Concupiscence, by the secret Grace of God, is changed to Wine of the best Taste. But why search we so many Proofs in so clear a Thing? especially,

---

[69] Jam. 1:17
[70] 1 Corn. 7:12
[71] Gen. 1:28
[72] Jn. 2

when that only Text is sufficient for all, where Christ says, Whom God has joined together., let no Man put asunder[73], the admirable Word! which none could have spoken, but the Word that was made Flesh! who thinks it not to have been abundantly sufficient, that God has joined the first of Mankind; and that the Bounty of so great a God is to be admired by all Men? But now we are taught from Truth itself, that those who are law fully married, are not rashly joined together; not by the Ceremonies of Men only, but by the invisible Presence and insensible Co-operation of God himself: And therefore, is it forbidden, that any should separate those whom God has joined together. O Word as full of Joy and Fears as it is of Admiration! Who should not rejoice, that God has so much Care over his Marriage, as to vouchsafe, not only to be present at it, but also to preside in it? Who should not tremble, whilst he is in Doubt how to use his Wife, whom he is not only bound to love, but also to live with, in such a Manner, as that he may be able to render her pure and immaculate to God, from whom he has received her?

Wherefore, seeing that God himself, as he says, joins all married People together; who believes not that he infuses Grace by Marriage? Does he join always, and give his Blessing but once? Why reassumes he the Office of joining, if we believe him not also to reassume that of Blessing? Or can we imagine, that the most holy Spirit, which is to be adored in Spirit and in Truth, should always exercise the Office of joining married People, for Care of carnal Copulation only? Indeed, as for that Matter, it should be sufficient that God leaves Man, like other Animals, to his own natural and corrupt Inclinations. There must be understood Something sure more holy than the Care of propagating the Flesh, which God performs in Marriage; and that, without all Doubt, is Grace; which is by the Prelate of all Sacraments infused into married People in consecrating Marriage.

Seeing therefore, we have, by so many Reasons, proved Grace to be conferred in Marriage; and that Marriage, which (as appears by the Words of the Apostle) is a Sign of a sacred Thing, (which Sign, is joined with Grace, as is already said) cannot be a bare Figure only; it follows then, that, in Despite of Luther, Marriage is a Sacrament; though it had not, (as it is) been so called by the Apostle.

But has any one, either Ancient or Modern, doubted to call Marriage a Sacrament, without being hissed at by the Church? In which alone, as Hugo de Sancto Victore mentions, is found a two-fold Sign: Tor Marriage itself is the Sacrament of the Society, which is in the Spirit between God and Man; but the Duty of Marriage is the Sacrament of that Society, which in the Flesh is between Christ and the Church. For if that (says he) which is in the Flesh, is great, much more that which is in the Spirit: And if God is rightly called in Scripture, a Bridegroom, and the Soul of Man the Bride, there is certainly Something betwixt God and the Soul; of which, what consists in Marriage betwixt Man and Woman, is the Sacrament, and Image. But perhaps, (to speak more expressly) that Society, which is exteriorly observed, according to the Contract in Marriage, is the Sacrament; and the mutual Love of the Souls, which is kept by an interchangeable Bond of conjugal Society and Alliance, is the Matter of the Sacrament.

---

[73] Matt. 19:6

And again; this same Love, by which Male and Female are spiritually united in the Sanctity of Wedlock, is the Sacrament and Sign of that Love, by which God is interiorly joined to the rational Soul, by Infusion of his Grace, and Participation of his Spirit. Thus far the Words of Hugo.

Wherefore, seeing that not only the public Faith of the Church, for so many Ages before us, and the ancient Fathers, remarkable for their virtuous Lives and Knowledge in Scripture; but also the blessed Apostle, St. Paul., Doctor of the Gentiles, have esteemed Marriage as a Sacrament, (which makes Wedlock honor able, and does by Grace, not only conserve the Bed unspotted from Adultery; but also washes away the Stains of Lust, turns Water into Wine, and procures a holy Pleasure of abstaining, even from lawful Pleasures.) I do not perceive what Luther can say to the Contrary; unless it is because Heretics (as St. Bernard saith) do still, according to their own Fancies, strive who shall exceed others, in endeavoring, with their viperous Teeth, to tear in Pieces the Sacrament of the Church, as the Bowels of their Mother.

CHAPTER XII
Of the Sacrament of Orders

In the Sacrament of Orders, Luther keeps no Manner of Order; but gathering together from here and there all the Treasuries of his Malice, he pours them out against it.

He shews how well his Mind is composed for Evil, if his Power were answerable thereto: He proposes many Things, and asserts and affirms the worst: But, satisfying himself by only saying, thus, and thus, he confirms Nothing at all, by any Manner of Reason. In which Proceeding his great Impudence appears, who, not vouchsafing to believe the whole Church, (without having Reasons for its Faith) does unreasonably require that he himself should be credited, without shewing any Reason at all; and that in Matters of such Nature, as he cannot tell what is to be believed, unless the Church teach him: And yet he desires to be believed, and that in such Sort, as to do it, is to confound and trample under Foot the whole Church: For what else aims he at, by endeavoring to take away the Holy Sacrament of Orders, then, by rendering the Ministers of the Church contemptible, he may procure, that the Sacraments of the Church may be also despised, and undervalued, as being ministered by the Hands of vile and unworthy Ministers: Which is the only Drift of his whole Work. And because Luther proceeds with no Order, in treating of Order; we will gather his Opinions here and there, that the Reader may have under one View that Heap of Evils; which being looked over, we need not take any great Pains, I suppose, to convince him, whose wicked Doctrine all Men may see tends directly to the Destruction of the Faith of Christ, by Infidelity. For what designs he else, who disputes that there is no Difference of Priesthood between the Laity, and Priest? that all Men are Priests alike: That all Men have the same Power, in what Sacrament soever: That the Ministry of the Sacraments is not given to the Priests, but by Consent of the Laity: That the Sacrament of Orders is Nothing else but the Custom of electing a Preacher in the Church: That he is not a Priest, who is not a Preacher, unless it be equivocally, as a painted Man, may be called a Man: That a Priest may be made a Layman again, when he pleases; because his priestly Character is Nothing: Moreover, that Order itself, which as a Sacrament, ordains some to be Clergymen, is merely and altogether a Fiction invented by Men, who understand Nothing of ecclesiastical Matters, of Priesthood, of the Ministry, of the Word, or of a Sacrament? Finally, this holy Priest, (whereby you may conjecture how chaste he himself is) makes it the greatest Error, and greatest Blindness imaginable, that Priests should undertake to lead a single Life. And when Christ praises those who have made themselves Eunuchs for the Kingdom of Heaven; this most filthy Antichrist compares them to the old idolatrous gelded Priests of the Heathen Sibyls. I know that this Catalogue of pernicious Opinions has long since wearied the Ears of the pious Reader; every one of which Opinions is more stuffed with Heresies, than the Trojan's Horse is reported to have been with armed Men.

But his denying Orders to be a Sacrament, is as it were the Fountain to all the rest; which, being once stopped up, the other small Springs must of Necessity become dry of themselves. This Sacrament (says he) is not known to the Church of Christ, but has been in vented by the Church of the Pope. In these few Words, are contained a great Heap of Absurdities and Lies: For he makes Distinction between Christ's Church, and the Pope's whereas the Pope is Christ's Vicar, in that, over which Christ is the Head. He says the Church has invented; when it has received it as already instituted, and therefore has not invented it. This Sacrament (he says) is unknown to the Church of Christ: Whereas it is most certain, that all Parts of the World, which have the true Faith of Christ, have Orders for a Sacrament: For if he could find some obscure Corner, (which I doubt he cannot) in which this Sacrament of Orders should not be known; yet ought not that Corner to be compared to the rest of the whole Church; which not only is subject to Christ, but also, for Christ's Sake, to Christ's only Vicar the Pope of Rome, and believes Orders to be a Sacrament.

Otherwise, if Luther persists in his Distinction of the Pope's Church, from Christ's-, and in saying that the one has Orders for a Sacrament, the other not; let him shew us the Church of Christ, which, contrary to the Faith of the Papal Church, (as he calls it) knows not the Sacrament of Order. In the meanwhile, it appears evidently, that, by asserting this Sacrament to be unknown to the Church of Christ, and that they are not of Christ's Church who are governed by the Pope; he separates, by both these Reasons, from Christ's Church, not only Rome, but also all Italy, Germany, Spain, France, Britain, and all other Nations, which obey the See of Rome; or have Orders for a Sacrament. Which People, being by him taken from the Church of Christ; it consequently follows, that he must either confess Christ's Church to be in no Place at all, or else, like the Donatists, he must reduce the Catholic Church to two or three Heretics whispering in a Corner.

But he draws out of his Shaft, as an inevitable Dart, That Grace is in no Place promised to this Sacrament; and that the New Testament makes not the least Mention of it: He says, that it is a ridiculous Thing to assert that for the Sacrament of God, which cannot anywhere be demonstrated to have been instituted by God. Nor is it lawful (says he) to assert any Thing to be of Divine Institution, which is not of Divine Ordinance; but we ought (says he) to endeavor to have all Things confirmed to us from clear Scripture.

We will see, by and by, whether no Mention is made at all of this Sacrament in the New Testament: For by the same Dart he expects to wound all the rest of the Sacraments; against which Dart, I will take the same Buckler or Shield which Luther himself confesses to be impenetrable.

His own Words are these: Truly the Church has this Faculty, that it can discern the Word of God, from the Word of Men; even as St. Augustine confesses, that he has believed the Gospel by the Motion of the Church s Authority; which told him that it was the Gospel. Wherefore, seeing that the Church, as Luther confesses, can discern the Word of God, from the Word of Men; it is certain it has not that Power, but from God; nor for any other Cause, then that it may not err in those Things, in which there ought to be no Error. It follows then, out of this Foundation he has laid for us, that the Church has from God, not only the Power of discerning God s Word from that of Mens, (which he allows) but also the Faculty of discerning betwixt divine and human Sense of Scripture. Otherwise, what should it avail the Church to know, by God s Teaching, the true Scripture from that which is false, if it could not distinguish between the false and true Sense of true Scripture? Finally, it follows, by the same Reason, that God instructs his Church, even in Things which are not written; lest it might, through Errors, embrace false Things for true ones: For that is no less dangerous than that it might admit the Writings of Men, for the Words of God, or draw a false Sense out of the Word of God; especially if it should take false Sacraments for true ones, and human Traditions for divine; nay, not only the Traditions of Men, but the Inventions of the Devil; if the Church of Christ, should, as Enchanters do, place its Hope in feigned and vain Signs of corporal Things. It appears, therefore, by Luther's confessing the Church to have a Faculty of discerning the Words of God from the Words of Men, that it has no less Power to discern betwixt divine Institutions, and the Traditions of Men. For, otherwise, the Error which we are to avoid, might as well arise from the one Side, as from the other. And Christ s Care, is not, that his Church may not err, after this or that Manner; but that it may not err in any Manner whatsoever. But it could by no Error commit a greater Injury to Christ, than in putting its Trust, which it ought to have in him alone, in Signs not supported by any Grace, but empty and void of all the Advantages of Faith. Therefore, the Church cannot err about the Sacraments of Faith; no more, I say, than in admitting Scripture, (in which Luther confesses her infallible) which, if it were other wise, many Absurdities should follow; and especially this, that almost all Opinions of the Church, in Matters of Faith, established these many past Ages, may be disputed after the Fancy of every new-fangled Heretic; which were the most ridiculous Thing imaginable. For, if Nothing must be certainly believed, but what is confirmed by Scripture; and that (as he says) by clear Testimonies of Scripture too; we must not only, not assert the perpetual Virginity of the blessed Virgin Mary, but also an unexhausted Materia will be furnished for battering the Church, at the Pleasure of every one who is minded to stir up new Sects, or renew the old one: For, there have been at any Time few or no Heretics, who would not pretend to Scripture, everyone disputing their new-broached Opinions to be confirmed by Scripture; or, (however agreeable to Scripture, because the contrary was not therein defined) disputing, that what was alleged against their Sects, was otherwise to be understood, then as the orthodox Church understood it: And lest it might be clearly brought against them, they either forged another Sense, or preferred some other Passages of Scripture, which seemed contrary to the former; troubling all Things in such Manner, as to make them seem ambiguous. If the public Faith of the Church had not withstood Arius, the Heretic, I know not if he should ever have wanted a Subject of Dispute out of Scripture.

Now, seeing we have proved, by Luther s own Fundamentals, that the Sacraments believed by the Church could not be instituted but by God himself, though Nothing were read thereof in Scripture: Let us see whether Scripture makes not some Mention of this Sacrament. Men do unanimously confess, (Luther only excepted) that the Apostles were by our Savior ordained Priests, at his last Supper; where it plainly appears, that Power was given them to consecrate the Body of Christ, which Power the Priest alone hath. But, says Luther, it is not a Sacrament, because there is no Grace promised therein. But pray, how, or whence has he this Knowledge? Because (says he) it is not read in Scripture! This is his usual Consequence: It is not written in the Gospels, therefore has it not been done by Christ: Which Form of reasoning the Evangelist overthrows, when he says, Many Things were done, which are not written in this Book[74]. But let us touch Luther yet a little closer. He confesses that the Eucharist is a Sacrament; and he were mad, if he did not; but where, pray, does he find in Scripture, that Grace is promised in that Sacrament? For he admits Nothing but Scripture, and that clear Scripture too. Let him read the Passages that treat of our Lord's Supper, and see if he can find in any of the Evangelists[75], that Grace is promised in the receiving of the Blessed Sacrament. We read that Christ said, this is my Blood, which shall be shed for many, to the Remission of Sins. whereby he signified, that he should redeem Mankind by his Passion upon the Cross. But when he said, this do in Remembrance of me. He promises no Grace, or Remission of Sins, to him that does this; that is, to the consecrated Priests, or to him that receives the Eucharist. NOT doth the Apostle, in his Epistle to the Corinthians[76], when he threatens Judgment to them that unworthily receive, make Mention of any Grace to him that receives it worthily. If any Thing in the 6th of St. John promise Grace to him that receives the Sacrament of our Lord's Body and Blood; yet can that make Nothing for Luther, because he denies the whole Chapter to have any Reference at all to the Eucharist. You see here, very plainly, that he cannot maintain that Promise of Grace, which he so fairly promised us, in his whole Work, as the sole Basis of the Sacrament, and in that only Sacrament which he admits; unless, besides the Words of Scripture, he has recourse (as it is necessary for him) to the Faith of the Church.

Wherefore; as it is sufficient for us to read in the Gospel, that the Power of consecrating the Sacrament, was given them to whom the Priests succeed; so is it likewise enough, that we read the Council of the Apostle to Timothy, that he impose not Hands rashly upon anyone? Which Passage plainly demonstrates, that the Ordination of Priests is not performed by the Consent of the Laity, (by which alone Luther affirms, that a Priest

---

[74] Jn. 22:25
[75] Matt. 26:28
[76] 1 Corn. 11:24

may be ordained,) but by the Ordination of a Bishop only: and that by a certain Imposition of Hands; in which God, through the exterior Sign, should infuse an interior Grace. Concerning which Grace, why should we not believe the Church of the Living God? which is, as the Apostle saith, The Ground and Pillar of Truth[77]; for Luther himself must certainly believe her concerning the Grace promised in the Eucharist; as the Promise of that Grace, or the giving of it without any Promise, is known in this Faith of the Church.

Indeed, I admire that any one should be so distracted as to doubt, whether Grace is given by the Sacrament of Orders to the Priest of the Gospel; whereas we may read many Places, that seem to signify that Grace was conferred on the Priests of the old Law; and that God saith, you shall anoint and sanctify Aaron and his Sons, that they may exercise to me the Office of Priesthood[78]. Otherwise, what should this exterior Sanctification have signified for the Honor of God, if God had not likewise infused Grace, by which they should be likewise interiorly sanctified; and that also through Christ; the Faith of whose coming, gave Force and Strength to precedent Sacraments, even as it made the Jews capable of obtaining eternal Salvation?

But if anyone will not admit, that Grace was conferred to the Priesthood of the Old Law; yet has he no Reason to deny the Infusion of Grace into the Priests of the Evangelical Law: Because now, through the Passion of Christ the Fullness of Grace is come. In the Acts of the Apostles, when St. Paul and Barnabas were set apart for that Work, to which the Holy Ghost has called them[79], they were not sent away, before they were first ordained by Imposition of Hands. But pray, why did the Apostles lay Hands on them? Was it to touch their Bodies in a vain Manner, without profiting their Souls by spiritual Grace? How then dares Luther affirm, that this Sacrament was unknown to the Church of Christ, which was used by the Apostles? But (says he) it was never called a Sacrament by any of the ancient Doctors, except Dionisius; for we read nothing at all in the other Fathers, of these Sacraments, neither did they think on the Name of Sacrament, whenever they spoke of these Things; for the Invention of Sacraments is new/ (says he.) An excellent Reason of Luther's I must confess, yet altogether false; and if it was true, yet could it avail nothing for his Purpose. For if the Ancients had not writ at all, of a Thing perhaps never disputed amongst them; or if, when they did write of it, they should signify it by its proper Name, and not by that common Name of Sacrament; should it then follow, as a necessary Consequence, that there has been no Order at all, or that it was not a Sacrament? For if any Body should call Baptism by the proper Name of Baptism, and should not add the Word Sacrament; shall it be therefore said, that he does not think Baptism to be a Sacrament? Moreover, if Dionisius only, amongst all the holy Fathers, should write Orders to be a Sacrament, that alone should be sufficient to destroy Luther's Objection; by which he intends to make People believe, that the Invention of Sacraments is new; for this Novelty is contradicted by his confessing it to be written by him, whom he acknowledges to be ancient: And this would be true, though St. Dionisius were such a Man, as sacrilegious Luther feigns him to be, saying, That he had almost no solid Learning in him: That none of the Things

---

[77] 1 Tim. 3:15
[78] Ex. 28:1
[79] Act. 13

he writ in his ecclesiastical Hierarchy, are proved by Authority, or Reason; but that they are all his own Inventions, and much like Dreams: That in his mystical Divinity, which some ignorant Divines (says Luther) so much extoll; he is pernicious; more like a Platonist than a Christian: In which (says he) you will not only, not learn who is Christ; but if you had known it before, you should lose your Belief of him: I speak (says he) by Experience; (By the Experiment, I suppose, of losing Christ there himself.) And further; Pray what performs he in his ecclesiastical Hierarchy, but only describes allegorically some ecclesiastical Rites Finally, that he might shew in how light a Matter St. Dionysius lost his Labor, do you think (says he) it should be difficult for me to sport with Allegories in whatsoever is credited? It should not be any hard Work for me to write a better Hierarchy than that of Dionysius is. Who can patiently endure to see the pious Labors of the holy Man so much abused by this angler, as if he were raging against some Heretic like himself? For he calls him illiterate and foolish, and one that writes not only Dreams, but also pernicious Doctrines, destroying Christ! All which Reproaches, are, notwithstanding, to the Glory of the holy Man, whose Works are all sufficiently demonstrated to be good, by their displeasing only a Man so wicked as this. For what Agreement can there be betwixt Light and Darkness, between Christ and Belial? His own wicked Brain was the Cause that he gained no Good by the pious Books of this holy Man: For Horatius writ truly; Unless the Vessel be sweet, whatsoever you put therein will become sour. In as much as he says, He could write a better Hierarchy, than that of St. Dionysius. pray let him brag of it when he has done it. In the meanwhile, he undertakes a Thing much more difficult, when he goes about to demolish that Hierarchy which is founded upon a solid Rock.

The Indignation we have conceived at that impious Fellow s casting such injurious Reproaches against the holy Man, has caused us somewhat to digress. But, as I begun to say, though St. Dionisius had been the Man that had taught holy Orders to have been a Sacrament; yet that is, however, sufficient to convince Luther, when he asserts the Invention of the Sacraments to be but a new Thing; since he not only confesses Dionisius to be ancient, but also that all the Christian World honors him for a Saint. So that Luther s Anger against him, is caused merely through Malice, which suffers him to brook nothing contrary to his wicked Heresies.

But now, that his Vanity in every Place may the more plainly appear; I will shew, that not only St. Dionisius, but also St. Gregory, and St. Augustine, (whom he falsely calls his Patron,) take Orders for a Sacrament. Moreover, this indefaceable Character (by him derided) though not called by that very Name; yet St. Jerome, in the Sacrament of Baptism, writes plainly enough of the Thing itself, to which also St. Augustine has had Regard, both in the Sacraments of Baptism and Orders. I will therefore begin with St. Jerome, of the Character of Baptism, that the Character of Orders may more evidently appear; which for its Indebility, both St. Augustine and St. Gregory compare with the Sacrament of Orders. St. Jerome, therefore, on these Words of St. Paul to the Ephesians, (Do not contristate the holy Spirit of God, in which you were signed in the Day of Redemption[80]) writes thus, but we have been signed with the Holy Ghost, that our Spirit and Soul may be sealed with the Signet of God, and that we may receive that

---

[80] Eph. 4:30

Image and Similitude, after which we were first created. This Seal of the Holy Ghost, according to the Words of our Savior, is stamped by God himself: For, says he, this has God the Father signed[81] and a little after, He is therefore signed, that he may keep the Seal; and that he may, in the Day of Redemption, shew it pure, sincere, and unchanged: that therefore he may receive his Reward with those who are redeemed. Amongst all those, who have ever writ of the Character of Sacraments, none could have more plainly expressed the Character, whereby God Almighty signs the Soul through the Sacraments, then St. Jerome has done in these Words; not by human Fiction (as Luther, that execrable Scoffer of Sacraments, feigns,) but by solid Testimonies of holy Scriptures.

For a Character is that Quality of the Soul, which God Almighty, (best known to himself, and to us in scrutable,) doth impress as a Seal, whereby to know his own Flock from Strangers: Which Character, though they stain it with Vices, and turn it from White to Black, from Perfect to Imperfect, from most Pure to Impure; yet can they never so raze it out, but that in the Day of Judgment, those therewith signed, will be known to all the World, to be of his Flock, who has marked them with that Signet : Which is the only Reason, why the Church so constantly observes; that, whereas she renews so often other Sacraments, as the Eucharist, Penance, Marriage, Extreme Unction; yet never suffers Baptism, Confirmation, and Holy Orders to be renewed; having learned from the Holy Ghost, that the Seal of the Character is imprinted in these Sacraments, so that it cannot be defaced, therefore ought not to be iterated.

But that it may more evidently appear, that Orders are, in this Case, like to Baptism; let us hear St. Gregory, it is (says he) a ridiculous Thing to say, that he who has received Holy Orders, ought to receive them again; for, as he who has once been baptized, ought not to be baptized again; so he, who has been once consecrated, ought not again to be consecrated in the same Degree of Orders. You see that the Church suffers not the Sacrament of Orders to be iterated, any more than that of Baptism, by Reason of its indelible Character. But to shut Luther s Mouth, who calls that Character a feigned Thing, and that St. Dionysius was the only Man, of all the ancient Fathers, that catted Holy Orders a Sacrament: We will, as we have promised, give you St. Augustine s Words; who, in treating of Baptism and Holy Orders, speaks thus; They are both Sacraments, and given to Man after certain Consecration; the one at his Baptism, the other when he receives Holy Orders: Therefore, it is not lawful in the Holy Catholic Church to iterate either of them. For when any heretical Minister is received into the Church, for the Good of Peace; if, after the Error of Schism is corrected, it should seem necessary, he should exercise the same Office, which he had before: Yet is he not to be ordained again; for, as Baptism remains entire in them, so Orders also; because the Vice consisted in the Separation, not in the Sacraments, which are the same, where-ever they are: And a little after, Injury must be done to neither of the two Sacraments. And of the Sacrament of Orders, he adds, That, as he that breaks off from Unity, has it not rightly, yet has it; so likewise, he does not rightly give it, yet gives it: And returning again to both, it hinders them not (says he) from being the Sacraments of Christ and his Church; because Heretics and wicked Persons use them unlawfully; but these Men

---

[81] Jn. 6:27

are to be corrected, and punished, and the Sacraments to be acknowledged and venerated. You see how void of Truth it is, what Luther so boldly boasts, viz. That the Sacrament of Holy Orders was unknown to the Church of Christ: That Character is an idle Fiction; That the Invention of Sacraments is a new Thing: That Holy Orders were no Sacrament among the Ancients. You see Nothing of what he has said, but has been rejected by the Testimony of such Persons, as he cannot separate from the Church of Christ; for they were illustrious therein by Doctrine of Faith and exemplary Lives; nor can he reckon them among the Moderns, if a thousand Years be not with him as one Day[82]. Notwithstanding this, he opposes himself against all the reasons, Authority, and Faith of all, by this one Argument: We are all Priests (says he) according to that of St. Peter. Ye are all a royal Priesthood, and priestly Kingdom[83]; but as one cannot be more a Man than another; so one can be no more a Priest than another: Those, therefore, who are called Priests, are no other but Lay-men, chosen by the only Consent of the People, or elected by the Bishop, not without the People: For to preach and ordain, are Nothing but mere Ministry, without any Thing of Sacrament. We have not only faithfully repeated his Argument, but also freely set down whatever may support him: And yet who would not laugh at this doltish Divine? For, if the Order of Priesthood is therefore Nothing, because every Christian is a Priest; by the same reason it will follow, that Christ had Nothing above Saul: For David said of Saul, *Peccavi tangens Christum Domini*; I have sinned in touching (Chris tum) the Anointed of our Lord: Or that Christ had Nothing above them, of whom it is said, *Nolite tangere Christos meos*; Touch not mine anointed: Finally, that God had Nothing above all those of whom he said by the Prophet, I have said ye are Gods, and are all the Sons of the most High. In a Word, all Christians are Kings in the same Manner that they are Priests: For it is not only said, Ye are a royal Priesthood; but also, a priestly Kingdom. Let us diligently observe what the Serpent designs, who, I suppose, is craftier than to think this Argument of any Consequence, but only licks, that he may afterwards bite: He extols the Laity to the Priesthood, for this only Reason, that he may reduce Priests to the Rank of the Laity; denying Priesthood to be a Sacrament, but only a Custom of electing a Preacher; and saying, that he who preaches, is no more a Priest, than the other; nay, no more a Priest, than a painted Man, is a Man. Contrary to St. Paul, who, writing to Timothy, says, The Priests that rule well, are worthy of double Honor, especially such as labor in the Word and Doctrine[84] The Apostle, by this, evidently teaches, that though those are most worthy of double Honor, who, being Priests, do labor in the Word and Doctrine: Yet those who perform not This, but can only govern well, are also Priests; and merit double Honor. Otherwise, he would not have said, especially those who labor in the Word and Doctrine; but only such as labor therein.

Furthermore, that Luther may not be able to hold what he says, viz. That the Priest's Office is nothing but to preach to the People: For to say Mass (says he) is nothing but to receive the Communion for himself: I say, that it may appear how false this is; let us again hear the Apostles Words, Every Priest (says he) that is taken out from amongst Men, is constituted for Men, in the Things which belong to God, that he may offer

---

[82] Ps. 89:4
[83] 1 Pet. 2:9
[84] 1 Tim. 5:17

Gifts and Sacrifices for their Sins[85]. Does not this plainly shew us that a Priest's Duty requires from him, to offer Sacrifices to God for Men? Though writing to the Hebrews, (yet not willing, that Christians should be any Thing Jewish,) it is evident that it is spoken of the Priesthood of both Laws; so that Luther is twice pressed by this Testimony: For he also teaches Mass to be a Sacrifice, and to be offered for the People: Seeing the Church offers no other; and he teacheth, that the Duty of offering it, is the chief Part of the Priest's Charge. And truly if Luther s Words were not false, how easily may you see it to follow; that since none but a Priest can consecrate our Lord's Body: of so many Thousand Priests, that have not the Gift of Preaching, if they were not truly Priests, but only equivocally so called, as a painted Man is called a Man; then would almost all the Christian World have no other God, or People but Idolaters, adoring Bread for Christ, and bending their Knees to Baal.

In the Right of electing, as he calls it, he attributes the chief Power to the People; for though in one Place; he seems to give this Rite promiscuously to the Bishop and People, (when he says, that although it is certain all Christians are equally Priests, and that they have a like Power in all the Sacraments: Yet that none can lawfully exercise this Power, without the Consent of the Congregation, or the Vocation of a Superior. Yet, in another Place, he gives the greatest Right to the People when, speaking of Priests, he says, who, if they were compelled to admit all of us, who have been baptized equally to be Priests, as indeed we are; and that the Ministry is only given to them by our Consent; they should know also, that they have no Right of ruling over us, but what we admit them of our own free Will. Which two Places being compared together, shews his Opinion to be, That the People, without the Bishop, but not the Bishop without the People, can ordain Priests; as appears by his saying, That the Ministry only is permitted to the Priests, and that not without the Consent of the People: Which if true, a Priest cannot be ordained, without the People's Consent; by which alone, he says, That Bishops were formerly made Rulers of the Church.

It cannot be denied, (says he) that the true Churches were formerly governed by Elders, without the Ordinations and Consecrations; being chosen to this, by Reason of their Age and long Experience in Things of that Kind. Pray let him shew us where he finds these Things? For my Part, I do not think them to be true. For, if every Layman hath equal Power over any of the Sacraments, with a Priest; and if the Order of Priest hood stands for Nothing, why writes the Apostle thus to Timothy, Neglect not the Grace which is in thee, and which has been given thee by Prophesy, by the Imposition of the Hands of the Presbytery[86]? and in another Place, to the same, I admonish thee, that thou stir up the Grace of God that is in thee, by the Imposition of my Hands[87]. Again, Impose Hands suddenly on no Man, neither be thou Partakers of other Men's Sins[88]. Finally, these are the Words of the Apostle to Titus; For this Cause left I thee in Crete, that thou shouldest correct the Things that are wanting; and constitute Priests in the Cities, even as I have appointed thee[89].

---

[85] Heb. 5:1
[86] 1 Tim. 4:14
[87] 1 Tim. 1:6
[88] 1 Tim. 5:22
[89] Tit. 1:5

Now Reader, you have, in a few Words, seen some Passages of the Apostle, by comparing of which, you may easily discover, that whatsoever Luther has thus disorderly vented against Order, are mere Fictions and Lies: For what he says, is done by the People's Consent, St. Paul shews to be done by the Bishop, while he says, He has left him (Titus) at Crete, to that End that he should ordain Priests in the Cities, and that not rashly, but as he himself, when present, had appointed. You see, by this, that Priests are made by Imposition of Hands. And that it may not be doubted that Grace is also given at the same Time; you see, that it is conferred by Imposition of Hands: Stir up (says he,) the Grace of God; which has been given thee by the Imposition of my Hands[90], and this also, Neglect not the Grace which is in thee, and which has been given thee through Prophesy, by Imposition of the Hands of the Presbytery[91] Take Notice of these Things 1 admire that Luther is not ashamed to deny the Sacrament of Holy Orders, as he is not ignorant that the Words of St. Paul are in every Man's Hands; which teach, that a Priest cannot be ordained but by a Bishop, and not without Consecration: In which both the corporeal Sign is adhibited, and so much spiritual Grace infused, that he who is consecrated, not only receives the Holy Ghost for himself, but also the Power of imparting it to others. Can that which the Apostle has writ be new, though it is so affirmed by Luther? How can it be unknown to the Church, which is, and has at all Times been, read through the universal Church of Christ? By these Things, it is manifest, that of all that Luther has railed out so confidently against Holy Orders, not one Syllable is true, but all the mere lying Inventions of his Malice.

---

[90] 1 Tim. 1:6
[91] 1 Tim. 4:14-15

CHAPTER XIII
Of the Sacrament of Extreme Unction

Tiff this Sacrament of Extreme Unction; that Luther might be twice derided himself, he twice scoffs the Church: First, because Divines, (says he) do call this Unction a Sacrament; (as if those he calls Divines, were the only Men who call it a Sacrament.) Again, because they call it Extreme; to which, as to the second, he himself objects, after a joking Manner, what he can never answer in earnest: For it may be rightly called Extreme, as being the last of four. Afterwards, to shew that it is no Sacrament, himself first objects, what he foresees everybody will object against him, viz. the Words of St. James the Apostle, if any be sick amongst you, let him send for the Priests of the Church, and let them pray over him, anointing him with Oil, in the Name of our Lord: And the Prayers of the Faithful will save the Sick, and our Lord will raise him up; and if he be in Sins, they shall be forgiven him[92]. These Words, (which, according to his own Definition, most apparently testify Extreme Unction to be a Sacrament, as wanting neither a visible Sign, nor Promise of Grace) he immediately begins, with most impudent Confidence, to deride; as if they were of no Manner of Force. For my Part, (says he) I say, that if ever there was Folly acted, it is especially in this Place. And I, again on the Contrary do affirm, that if ever Luther was mad at any Time, (as indeed his Madness appears almost in every Place,) he is certainly distracted here, in the Sacrament of Extreme Unction, to an extreme Height of Madness. I omit (says he) saying that many do probably assert this not to be the Epistle of the Apostle St. James, nor worthy an apostolic Spirit, though by Custom, whosoever it be, it has obtained Authority: Yet if it were certainly written by the Apostle St. James, I should say that it is not lawful for an Apostle to institute a Sacrament by his own Authority; that is, to give a divine Promise, with a Sign joined thereunto: This belongs to Christ alone. So that St. Paul says that he received from our Lord the Sacrament of the Eucharist; and that he was sent, not to baptize, but to preach the Gospel: But of the Sacrament of Extreme Unction we read nowhere in the Gospel. You see how he endeavors here, two Ways, to weaken the Words of the Apostle. First, he will not have the Epistle to have

---

[92] Jam. 5:14-15

been writ by the Apostle. Secondly, though it was by him written; yet will he not have the Apostle to have Authority of instituting Sacraments. Although he has proposed these two Things in a few Words, and passes hastily on to some other; yet are they the chief Weapons, by which he intends to destroy this Sacrament; for what else he says, are but Trifles, whereby he takes Occasion to laugh, as if the Church did not well in observing this Sacrament. But these two do come both to the same Thing: For if the Epistle had not been writ by the Apostle, or is not worthy an apostolical Spirit; or if, for the Apostle s giving this Unction for a Sacrament, it be not the more approved to be one: Yet it should follow plainly, that nothing could be affected by these Words. If he had said, that it was formerly doubted whose Epistle this was, he had said truly; for the Church admits Nothing rashly, it discusses everything diligently: And this it doth, that everything it receives, may be had for greater Certainty; though it were only directed by human Policy. But when he says, that many do assert this Epistle, not only, not to be of the Apostle's Writing; but also, unworthy of an apostolical Spirit; and that they not only assert, but probably assert this; it is more than probable, he cannot prove what he says; otherwise let him name some of these many Persons; who if they be of the Church, I suppose they are not so many, nor of so great Authority, as to be able to stand out against the whole Church. But as yet he has produced none: I will therefore bring one who may suffice against his many, to wit, St. Jerome; who, in holy Scriptures, was the most learned of his Time, and has as exactly distinguished between dubious and real Things, as could be possible. This great Man, after he had for some Time remained doubtful, of the Epistle of St. Paul, (and that only at such Time as it was not confirmed by a full Consent of the whole Church.) Yet he pronounces the Epistle of St. James to be undoubtedly of his own Writing: His Words are these, St. James, St. Peter, St. Jude, and St. John, have published seven Epistles, as mystical, as they are succinct and short; yea, likewise long; short in Words, and long in Sentences, so that there are not many, who would not be blinded in the reading them. The same St. Jerome, speaks thus of the seven canonical Epistles, the first of them is one St. James's, the second, of St. Peter's, three of St. John's, one of St. Jude's: You see how this Father has the same Opinion of St. James s Epistle that he has of St. Peter's; nor does he think it unworthy an apostolical Spirit: Truly if Luther had brought us any Reasons why this Epistle must not be accounted St. James s, (though of some other Person, who should speak in the same Spirit,) yet should he be in some Sort tolerable. But now he says, it is not probable it should be St. James's, because it is unworthy an apostolical Spirit: In which Thing, I will bring no Objections, but Luther's own against Luther; for none did ever more frequently and strongly contradict himself, than Luther. In the Sacrament of holy Order, he says, The Church has Power given her to discern the Word of God, from the Words of Men. How then does he say, that this Epistle is unworthy an apostolical spirit, which the Church whose Judgment (as himself confesses) cannot err in this, has judged it to be full of apostolical Spirit? Wherefore, he has now, by his own Wisdom, so hemmed himself in on all Sides, that he must necessarily consent that this Epistle belongs to the Apostle, contrary to what he has affirmed to be probable; or, that the Church can err in distinguishing Scripture, which before he denied. If he says that the Church has approved, as worthy of an apostolical Spirit, what is unworthy, then is he a Blasphemer against the Church: If he holds that the Apostle has writ what is unworthy an Apostle, then is he a Blasphemer against the Apostle. We have therefore sufficiently confuted this: Indeed, he has sufficiently confuted himself, in denying the Epistle to belong to the Apostle, or to be worthy an apostolical Spirit. Now come we to that, in which, like a valiant Man, he openly sets upon the Apostle himself, saying, that though it was of the Apostle's Writing, yet it is not lawful for an Apostle to institute a Sacrament by his own Authority; that is, to give a divine Promise, with a Sign thereunto adjoined: For this (says he) belongs to Christ alone. O this happy Age! in which Luther, this new Doctor of the Gentiles, is risen, who will seem himself to follow the Example of St. Paul, by resisting an Apostle to his Face[93], as not going the right Way to the Gospel of Christ, but (which is more than if he should teach the Gentiles to Judaize) arrogating to himself the Power of promising Grace, and instituting Sacraments; usurping in that the Power of Christ; like the proud and traitorous Angel, who said it. I will establish my Throne in the North, and be like to the Most High[94]. The Pope has no great Cause of being vexed at his Reproaches, who charges such enormous Crimes upon the Apostle himself: For, since it is certain this Epistle belongs to the Apostle; what else does he then, but manifestly accuse the Apostle of having (without Authority, and against all Right) instituted this Sacrament? Nay, when he denies the Epistle to belong to the Apostle (lest he should leave off his Calumny,) he professes, that he would say as much, if It was of the Apostle s own Writing! Indeed, though some think, that the Apostle received Power of instituting Sacraments, (not without the Power of the Holy Ghost, which God sent them at Pentecost, and of which Christ had foretold, The Holy Ghost which I will send unto you, He shall teach you all Things[95].) Yet shall not I dispute it at this Time, whether an Apostle has such Power or no, because it is now not necessary to dispute it. But seeing it is evident, that the Apostle gives us this Unction as a Sacrament, I do not doubt, but it is really a Sacrament; and that the Apostle was not so impiously arrogant, as to give the People, for a Sacrament, what was in Reality no such Thing. But if the Apostle had not the Power of instituting this Sacrament himself, then has he delivered it to the People in these Words, as he received it from Christ, who, as he would notify to the World some Things by St. Matthew, some by St. Luke, some by St. John, and some by the Apostle St. Paul; why is it not possible he should be pleased to make known some Things unto us, by the Apostle St. James.

Luther having thus strenuously behaved himself against the Apostle, begins now altogether to turn himself against the Church: Which (as he says) abuseth the Words of the Apostle, in not administering this Unction to the Sick, but when at the Point of Death: Whereas St. James says, if any be sick, not if any be dying. As if the Church sinned in not exhibiting in considerately, in every light Fever, (contracted, perhaps, by too much Drinking) so great a Thing as a Sacrament; or, in not attributing to herself a Miracle in healing such Disease, as either Sleep, or Abstinence can cure; that it may not be doubted, though the Apostle writes sick, that yet he did not mean a Man in every light Sickness, but troubled with such Sickness, as, if cured, may shew to be taken away by Virtue of the Sacrament; and that this Sacrament is not to be adhibited, but in great Sickness; appears by all the Prayers which are said over the sick Person, which, no Doubt, are very ancient, and not of the new Invention of those he calls Divines. And though they do not promise an assured Health of the Body, yet do they not despair of Health; nor do they (as Luther says,) come to such only, as are sure undoubtedly to die;

---

[93] Gal. 2:11-14
[94] Is. 14:13-14
[95] Jn. 14:26

for it should be in vain to pray for his Health, if they were sure of his Death.

Therefore, the Church's Intention, is, not (as he impertinently cavils) that this should be the last Sacrament, although it is so called, but on the Contrary, and that the sick Person may recover his Health; which, if God is not pleased he should; yet that is no Prejudice to the Force and Virtue of the Sacrament, which tends more to the curing of the Soul, than to the Health of the Body. As for Luther s Reason, concerning the Efficacy of the Sign, it is altogether without Reason or Efficacy: If that Unction be (says he) a Sacrament, it ought, without Doubt, to be an effectual Sign of what it promises; but it promises the Health and Recovery of the Sick, as appears by the Words, The Prayers of the Faithful shall save the Sick, and our Lord will raise him: Yet who sees not but this Promise is fulfilled in very few? What shall we say then? (says he), For either the Apostle speaks false in this Promise, or else this Unction is no Sacrament; for a sacramental Promise is certain, but this, for the most Part, fails. It appears by this only Argument, that Luther cares not much how open his Calumnies are, so that he can but, under some Pretext of Truth, impose upon the Unwary: For he shames not to object against the Divines, (as said by them,) what they never spoke: A Sacrament (says he) is, according to their Sayings, an effectual Sign of what it promiseth; but this Sacrament gives not the Health of the Body, which it promiseth. But Divines say no such Thing; they say it is an effectual Sign of Grace, defining it thus, A Sacrament is a visible Sign of invisible Grace: They do not speak of the Health of the Body, which may be given without Grace. So that when he says, that if Unction be a Sacrament, the Apostle should lye; it is Luther himself that lyeth: For the Sacrament, in as much as it is a Sacrament promiseth not the Health of the Body, but of the Soul, by a corporeal Sign. Nevertheless, Luther comprehends, under the same Lye, not only the Apostle, but Christ himself, though Unction were no Sacrament: For the Words and Promise ought to be true also, without the Sacrament. Therefore, when the Apostle says, The Sick shall be healed by Unction and Prayers; And when Christ says, These Signs shall follow those that

believe in him, to wit, that they should lay Hands on the Sick, and they should be healed[96]; who sees not that sometimes these Things are performed, but not always? Neither yet are they false who promised them: For, in whatsoever Words they promised corporeal Things; yet everybody knows, they never promised them to be perpetual, when the Body, in which they are to be done, cannot last always. But spiritual Things are here to be understood, because the Spirit is to live forever. For Luther's Sentence (which exacts from the Divines, that, if Unction is a Sacrament, it may always cure, that may not be an ineffectual Sign) undertakes to prove that it cannot be a Sacrament, if it renders not the Body immortal: Which, nevertheless, he himself promises to be done by the Prayers of good Men, without the least staggering in Faith: For, (says he) There is no Doubt, but at this Day, as many as we please may be cured: Which, if true, such a Faith as this may preserve Man immortal: For, seeing this may be done by Faith, not only Sometimes, but, as he affirms, always, if Faith be stable and undoubtful; it is probable indeed, if any one ever meet with such a Faith: And doubtless Luther was a Man of such Faith, (having so much thereof, that in Favor of it, in many Places, he

---

[96] Mar. 16:17-18

almost bids Defiance to good Works; being likewise one to whom God has revealed so many, and so great Mysteries, and who erects a new Church, for which Miracles are absolutely necessary) it is therefore likely that Luther can perform abundantly whatever can be done by Faith. If this be true, I wonder he cures not every dying Person! We look for News daily from Germany of his raising the Dead: Yet, for all this, we hear that not only none are cured by him, but that many good and innocent Priests are killed, (by his Adherents) and cruelly murthered for his Sake; that, by his Example, he may teach, That Holy Order is nothing: That Character is a Fiction: That David was timorous for repenting himself to have touched the Lord's Anointed[97].

These are Luther s Cures, wrought by his great Faith, without good Works. For, seeing he kills, and cures not; it appears plainly, (as he says, That Prayers are to be made not only by Faith, but also by good Men/) that Luther, not being a good Man, can therefore cure no Body himself. This Unction, he says, is no Sacrament, because it does not always heal the Body: But himself is a holy Man, by whom, as it is reported, the Body is killed, and certainly Souls are killed. St. James writes nothing worthy an apostolic Spirit; but Luther writes everything worthy such Spirit, and discerns Things unworthy thereof, and that against the whole Church: which, as he acknowledges, cannot be deceived in discerning such Scripture. In which Thing, when I had read St. James s Epistle, and saw so many Things worthy an apostolic Spirit therein, (as the Joy in overcoming Temptations, Patience in Adversity, Wisdom to be begged from God, hopes to be placed in God without staggering, with many such like; all which are read in the Apostle) I much wonder what Reason Luther had to think them unworthy to have been writ by an Apostle. But perhaps Luther would that the Apostle had writ such Things as these, to wit, That Mass is not profitable to the People, that Order is a vain Fiction; and such like, as himself writes; which are all Things worthy an apostolic Spirit. But though, as I said, I admired why Luther should be so much displeased at St. James s Epistle; yet, having read it more attentively, I wonder not at all: For, by the Apostle's Writings, I find that he so narrowly touches Luther every-where, as if, by his prophetic Spirit, he had plainly foreseen him. For, when Luther under the Pretext of Faith, despises good Works; St. James, on the other Side, disputes, by reason, Scripture, and Example, that Faith without Works, is dead: Nor is it in one Place alone, that by bitter Words, he resists that prattling Petulancy of Luther: If any one (says he) esteem himself religious, not bridling his Tongue, but seducing his own Heart, his Religion is vain[98]. Besides Luther frets at this, which he sees very fitly may be applied to his own Tongue. The Tongue is a restless Evil, full of deadly Poison[99],Finally, he perceives that what the Apostle has writ against contentious Persons, is truly spoken against his own Opinions: For (says the Apostle) who is wise and well-disciplined among you? Let him shew forth his Works by a good Conversation, in the Meekness of Wisdom; because, if you have the Zeal of Souls, and Contentions be in your Hearts, do not glory, being Liars against the Truth. For this is not Wisdom descending from above, from the Father of Lights, but an earthly, beastly, and diabolical Wisdom: For where Zeal is joined with Contention, there also is Inconstancy, and every naughty Work. But the Wisdom which is from above, is first of all shamefaced, then peaceable, modest, compliable, agreeing

---

[97] 1 Ki. 26:11-23
[98] Jam. 1:26
[99] Jam. 1:8

with good Things, full of Mercy and good Works, judging with Dissimulation: And the Fruit of Justice is sown in Peace to the Workers of Peace[100].

These, gentle Reader, are the Words which move Luther to Wrath against the Apostle: These, I say, are the Words whereby the Apostle as openly touches Luther's Petulancy, Railings, wicked and contentious Opinions; even as if he had seen him, and read his Words. I question not but his Epistle, though never so much despised by Luther, will sufficiently prove to all Christians the Sacrament of Extreme-Unction; nor shall Luther be ever so powerful, as to be able to abolish any Sacrament, which, for the Salvation of the Faithful, has been received by the Church, against which the Gates of Hell shall never prevail; much less this single Brother, who is but a sooty Wicket of Hell.

We have in this little Book, courteous Reader, clearly demonstrated, I hope, how absurdly and impiously Luther has handled the Holy Sacraments: For, though we have not touched all Things contained in his Book; yet so far as was necessary to defend the Sacraments, (which only was our design) I suppose I have treated, though not so sufficiently as might have been done, yet more than is even necessary; insomuch that it behoves me not to insist any longer thereupon; else were it no hard Matter to enrich this Discourse with more plentiful Arguments, Laws, and Sentences of the Holy Fathers, and Scripture itself, if it were not in vain, upon Luther's Account, and for others more than necessary; for it is as easy for the Ethiopian to change his color, or the Leopard his spots, as for Luther to be converted by teaching. But that others may understand how false and wicked his Doctrine is, lest they might be so far deceived as to have a good Opinion of him; I doubt not but in all Parts, there are very learned Men, though I had said Nothing at all of this Matter, who have much more clearly discovered the same, than can be shewn by me. And if there be any who desire to know this strange Work of his, I think I have sufficiently made it apparent to them. For, seeing by what has been said, it is evident to all Men what sacrilegious Opinions he has of the Sacrament of our Lord's Body, (from which the Sanctity of all the other Sacraments flows) who would have doubted, if I had said Nothing else, how unworthily, without Scruple, he treats all the rest of the Sacraments? Which, as you have seen, he has handled in such Sort, that he abolishes and destroys them all, except Baptism alone; and that too, he has abused and deprived of all Grace; leaving it for no other End, then in a Contumely of Penance; in some, denying the Sign, in others, the Matter itself: Neither proves he any Thing in this so great a Matter; nor brings he any Thing in Confirmation of his Doctrine; contenting himself in only denying whatever the Church admits. What everybody believes, he alone, by his vain Reason, laughs at; denouncing himself to admit Nothing, but clear and evident Scriptures: And these too, if alleged by any against him, he either evades by some private Exposition of his own, or else denies them to belong to their own Authors. None of the Doctors are so ancient, none so holy, none of so great Authority in treating of Holy Writ: But this new Doctor, this little Saint, this Man of Learning; rejects with great Authority. Seeing therefore he despiseth all Men, and believes none, he ought not to take it ill, if everybody discredits him again. I am so far from intending to hold any further Dispute with him, that I almost repent myself of what I have already argued against him. For what avails it to

---

[100] Jam. 3:13

dispute against a Man, who disagrees with everyone, even with himself? who affirms in one Place, what he denies in another; denying what he presently affirms; who, if you object Faith, combats by reason; if you touch him with Reason, pretends Faith; if you allege Philosophers, he flies to Scripture; if you propound Scripture, he trifles with Sophistry; who is ashamed of Nothing, fears none, and thinks himself under no Law; who contemns the ancient Doctors of the Church, and derides the new ones in the highest Degree; loads with Reproaches the chief Bishop of the Church: Finally, he so undervalues the Customs, Doctrine, Manners, Laws, Decrees, and Faith of the Church; yea, the whole Church itself; that he almost denies there is any such Thing as a Church; except perhaps such a one as himself makes up of two or three Heretics, of whom himself is Chief. Wherefore, since he is such a one, as will have no solid or certain Principle betwixt himself and his Adversary; but requires to be free in whatever pleases him, and as often as it pleases him lawfully to assert or deny; when, neither Reason, Scripture, Custom, Laws, human or divine Authority, binds him: I

thought it not fit to dispute any longer with him, nor to contend, by painful Reason, against his Heresies, which he confirms by no Reason. But I rather advise all Christians, that, as the most exterminating of Plagues, they shun him, who endeavors to bring into the Church of Christ such foul Prodigies, being the very Doctrine of Antichrist. For, if he, who studies to move a Schism in any one Thing, is to be extirpated with all Care; with what great Endeavors is he to be rooted out, who, not only goes about to sew Dissention, to stir up the People against the chief Bishop, Children against their Parents, Christians against the Vicar of Christ; finally, who endeavors to dissolve by his Tumults, Brawls and Contentions, the whole Church of Christ, which he, in the Time of his precious Death, has bound together by the Bond of Charity and Love; and also to destroy, profane and pollute, with a most execrable Mind, filthy Tongue, and detestable Touch, what is most sacred therein; who, if he did but give any Hopes of Cure in himself, or any Sign of Amendment, he would thereby move all People to regard Disposition, and to endeavor, by all good Means possible, to heal him, and to restore him to Soundness of Mind, that he might again, revoke the Heresies he has broached. But indeed, as yet, I see in him all the Signs that precede Death: I am not so much moved to think thus, by Reason of his Disease, though never so mortal; as by his admitting no Medicine, nor of any manual Operation of the Chyrurgion: For how can he be cured, who will not suffer himself to be handled? Or in what Manner is he to be dealt withal; who, if you teach him, trifles with you? If you advise him, is angry? If you exhort him, resists? If in any Thing you would appease him, is incensed? If you resist him, is mad? Otherwise, if he could be cured, what has the pious Vicar of Christ omitted, who, following the Example of a good Shepherd, would seek, find, take on his Shoulders, and bring home to the Fold this lost Sheep? But, alas! the greediest Wolf of Hell has surprised him, devoured and swallowed him down into the lowest Part of his Belly, where he lies half alive, and half dead in Death: And whilst the pious Pastor calls him, and bewails his Loss, he belches out of the filthy Mouth of the hellish Wolf these foul Inveighings, which the Ears of the whole Flock do detest, disdain, and abhor.

For, first of all, being unprovoked in any Kind, he proposed some Articles of Indulgences; in which, (under Pretense of Godliness,) he most impiously defamed the Chief Bishop: Afterwards, that he might under Pretense of Honor and Duty, cast on the Pope the greater Aspersion, he transmitted them to Rome, as if submitting himself to the Pope's Judgment; but he augmented them with Declarations, much worse than they were themselves; that it might appear to all Men, that the Pope would not be counselled by a good and pious Man, but derided by a knavish little Brother, as if so stupid as to hold for an Honor such a Contumely, as the like thereof had never before been heard. If the Pope deserved no ill, why has this degenerate Son, cast a false and undeserving Scandal on his Father? But if any Thing had been done at Rome, which needed reforming; yet if Luther had been (as he would be accounted) an honest Man, and zealous Christian, he should not have preferred his own private Glory before the public Good of all others, nor have desired to have had the Credit of a Scorner amongst the Wicked, laughing at the Nakedness of his sleeping Father[101], uncovering, and pointing thereto with his Finger; but, contrary-wise, would have covered the same, and would have more secretly advised him in his own Person by Letters, following the Example of the Apostle, who commands us not to deride or reproach our Superiors, but to seek of them[102]: Which if Luther had done, I doubt not but the more holy Pope, (so well is his great Benignity known to all Men) being awakened, should have blessed his Son Japhet; would have rendered him Thanks for his Piety; and would not have cursed him in his Anger; who has for born to curse him when he was mocked by him; but, pitying the miserable, and (more tender of a Son, than mindful of a Scoffer) has dealt with him by most honorable Men, in whose Presence he was not worthy to appear, that he might desist from his Iniquity: To which pious and wholesome Counsel, he was so far from obeying, that he not only derided the Legate, careful for his Salvation, but also immediately published another Book, in which he endeavored to overthrow the Pope's Power: After which, he was summoned to Rome, that he might either render Reasons of his Writings, or recant what he had inconsiderately written; having any Security imaginable offered him, that he should not undergo the Punishment which he deserved, with sufficient Expenses offered him for his Journey: Yet, for all this, this silly Brother, to shew his great Modesty and Obedience to the Pope, refused to go, unless in the Equipage of a King, and guarded by a warlike Army: But this wary Man made his Appeal to a general Council; yet not to every Council, but to such as should next meet in the Holy Ghost; that in whatsoever Council, he was condemned, he might deny the Holy Ghost to be present therein; for this holy and spiritual Man denies Him to be anywhere, but in his own Bosom: Wherefore, being oftentimes advised to repent of his Wickedness, the most conscientious Shepherd has at length been forced to cast out from the fold the Sheep suffering with an incurable Disease, lest the sound Sheep be corrupted by Contact, and to deplore the Death of his son Absalom, whose Life he was unable to save, while he sees him hanging from a Tree by his beautiful Hair, of which he had stupidly grown proud[103]. So Luther, realizing himself to be cast out from the Society of the Faithful, began to do what the lamented Wicked Ones do, who, when they have fallen into Contempt, contemn, [104]He has not uttered a Groan; he has not bewailed his Case, in which, exalted like Lucifer, like Lightning he has fallen[105] and wrought Damage; but having imitated the Despair of the Devil, himself a Devil too, that is having become a Calumniator, he has begun to rush into Blasphemies and Calumnies against the Pope, and, jealous of others

---

[101] Gen. 9:22
[102] 1 Tim. 5:1
[103] 2 Ki. 18:9
[104] Prov. 18:8, Gen. 3
[105] Lu. 10:18

faithful, like the old Serpent, to set up Nets of Infidelity, that he might get them to taste of the forbidden Tree of harmful Knowledge and to be driven out of the Paradise of the Church (whence he had fallen) onto an Earth bringing forth Thorns and Briars. I indeed bear very ill this Man's great Madness, and most lamentable State, and I wish that even now (God inspiring him by Grace) he may at length come to his Senses and be converted and live. And I do not wish this so much for his own Sake, (though for his too, as I wish all to be saved, if it be possible) as that at length being converted, and like the prodigal Son[106] returned to the Mercy of so benign a Father, and having confessed his Error, he may recall any whom he has made err.

But if he has sunken so deep in the Mire that now the Sink of Impiety and Despair shuts its Mouth upon him[107], let him blate, blaspheme, calumniate, act as a Madman, so that "he that is filthy, let him be filthy still."[108]

But I beseech and entreat all other Christians, and through the Bowels of Christ, (Whose Faith we profess,) to turn away their Ears from the impious Words and not to foster Schisms and Discords, especially at this Time when most particularly it behooves Christians to be concordant against the Enemies of Christ. Do not listen to the Insults and Detractions against the Vicar of Christ which the Fury of the little Monk spews up against the Pope; nor contaminate Breasts sacred to Christ with impious Heresies, for if one sews these he has no Charity, swells with vain Glory, loses his Reason, and burns with Envy. Finally, with what Feelings they would stand together against the Turks, against the Saracens, against anything Infidel anywhere, with the same Feelings they should stand together against this one little Monk weak in Strength, but in Temper more harmful than all Turks, all Saracens, all Infidels anywhere.

The End.

---

[106] Lu. 15
[107] Ps. 68
[108] Rev. 20:1